A Hunger So Wide and So Deep

A Hunger So Wide and So Deep

A Multiracial View of Women's Eating Problems

Becky W. Thompson

University of Minnesota Press

Minneapolis / London

The title of chapter 1 is taken from the composition "Oughta Be a Woman," music by Bernice Johnson Reagon, lyrics by June Jordan. Recorded by Sweet Honey in the Rock on "Good News," Flying Fish Records. Permission granted by Songtalk Publishing Company.

"Song for a Thin Sister" is reprinted from *Undersong: Chosen Poems Old and New*, revised ed., by Audre Lorde, by permission of W. W. Norton & Company, Inc. Copyright 1992, 1982, 1976, 1974, 1973, 1970, 1968 by Audre Lorde.

"Who Hurt You So, My Dear?" by Edna St. Vincent Millay. From *Collected Poems*, HarperCollins. Copyright 1954, 1982 by Norma Millay Ellis. Reprinted by permission of Elizabeth Barnett, literary executor.

Published by the University of Minnesota Press
111 Third Avenue South, Suite 290, Minneapolis, MN 55401-2520
Printed in the United States of America on acid-free paper
Fifth printing 2008

Library of Congress Cataloging-in-Publication Data
Thompson, Becky W.
    A hunger so wide and so deep : a multiracial view of women's eating problems / Becky W. Thompson.
      p. cm.
    Includes bibliographical references and index.
    ISBN 978-0-8166-2434-8 (hc : acid-free). – ISBN 978-0-8166-2435-5 (pb : acid-free)
    1. Eating disorders—Etiology. 2. Abused women—Mental health.
3. Minority women—Mental health. 4. Eating disorders—Etiology—Social aspects. 5. Eating disorders—Etiology—Political aspects.
6. Women—Social conditions. I. Title.
RC552.E18T456 1994
616.85'26071'082—dc20   93-43613

The University of Minnesota is an
equal-opportunity educator and employer.

I would hurl words into this darkness and wait for an echo, and if an echo sounded, no matter how faintly, I would send other words to tell, to march, to fight, to create a sense of the hunger for life that gnaws in us all, to keep alive in our hearts a sense of the inexpressibly human.

Richard Wright, American Hunger, *1977*

Contents

Acknowledgments

With a book whose origins reach back more than a decade, I have many people to thank. In the late 1970s and early 1980s I was extremely fortunate to work with several people—at Emma Goldman's Women's Health Center, Cook County Hospital in Chicago, the Santa Cruz Women's Health Center, and Janus Alcoholism Center—who believe that individual health is inextricably tied to the body politic and that universal health care is a must in a society that professes to be humane. Thanks especially to Carmella Woll, Bobbie Cohen, and Pam Pauly. When I moved to Boston I fell under the expert instruction of many women and men who attended the "Women's Hunger and Feeding Ourselves" workshops I facilitated at various New England universities from 1984 to 1990. The participants' honesty, courage, and knowledge sent me to the library stacks and later to conduct life history interviews, as I searched for an understanding of women's eating problems that underestimated neither their seriousness nor their meaning. As for the women who consented to let me interview them, this book simply would not be without them. I have carried memories of their stories, gestures, eyes, and insights around with me since we spoke. It was an honor to listen to and learn from them.

Writing this book has been a labor of love and sorrow. Along the way, I have been blessed with the companionship of many people who understood this and held me with their emotional, intellectual, and financial support: Sohaila Abdulali, Edward Abood, Michelle Baxter, Katie Cannon, Rose DeLuca, Mandy Devery, Estelle Disch, Lisa Hall, Evelynn Hammonds, Calvin Hernton, Susan Kosoff, Retha Powers, Kate Rushin, Sheryl Ruzek, Katherine Stern, and Evelyn C. White. As a doctoral student in sociology at Brandeis University, I was lucky to study with Maury Stein, Jacqui Alexander, Irv Zola, and Shulamit Reinharz, who taught me that intellectual breadth depends upon refusing to accept partitions between disciplines and that much of the best scholarship is rooted in a quest for justice.

While writing is necessarily solitary, there have been innumerable times when friends and family have scooped up drafts and counseled me onward. Thanks especially to Maggie Andersen, Lynn Davidman, Mary Gilfus, Nell Painter, and Sangeeta Tyagi for their love of language and belief in this project. I want to thank my mother for her passion for poetry and art and for refusing to let convention and bigotry stand in her way. My grandmother, a mainstay in my life, has taught me much about honor and beauty. Thanks to my sister, Ginny Onysko, for all the work she puts into raising her two open-hearted children, Ashley and Jeff, and for being my loving sister. She, my brother, and I held each other tight while we were growing up and it has made all the difference. I owe much to Sheila Averch for helping me get to the other side of some steep climbs and to Gayle Pemberton for her generous spirit, irreverence, and passion for music and writing.

Since I set my sights on putting this project out into the world, I have found intellectual and financial backing at key moments. A 1989 grant from the American Association of University Women gave me confidence that breathed life into an earlier version of this book. Through a Rockefeller Fellowship in the Afro-American Studies Program at Princeton University in 1992-93 I was given the chance to be in the company of an extraordinary group of scholars—Nell Painter, Wahneema Lubiano, Cornel West, Gayle Pemberton, Kevin Gaines, Toni Morrison, Howard Taylor, and Paula Giddings—while I wrote the book. They taught me much about the life of the mind and the power of intellectual thought as a tool of liberation. I owe much to Lisa Freeman, director of the University of Minnesota Press, who said "this is a take" and has made it her business to back the book wholeheartedly. I appreciate the sound and precise evaluations I received from three outside reviewers—Mary Zimmerman, Melanie Katzman, and Laura Brown. Lynn Marasco copyedited the manuscript with sensitivity and care. Thanks as well to Sharon Morrison and Susan

Wakefield for their proofreading skills, to Todd Orjala, Lisa Freeman's editorial assistant, and to Lorrie Oswald, the production coordinator for this book. I am also indebted to many whose work is a constant guide, especially Gloria Anzaldúa, Essex Hemphill, bell hooks, June Jordan, Martin Levine, Audre Lorde, Joan Nestle, and Bernice Johnson Reagon.

1 Making "a Way outa No Way"

Compulsive eating, bulimia, and anorexia have taken on complicated symbolic significance in late twentieth-century culture in the United States.[1] Those suffering from eating problems invariably are thought to be young, middle- to upper-class, heterosexual white women desperately trying to mold their figures to standards created by advertisers and clothing designers. The most popular terminology used to describe these problems is "eating disorder," which suggests that some psychological frailty or inadequacy is the agent of the illness. In short, those suffering from eating problems are thought to be decadent, self-absorbed, and heavily implicated in their own troubles. Such conceptions are misguided, short-sighted, and harmful. They are built on skewed assumptions about race, class, and sexuality that belittle the putative victims—white, middle-class, heterosexual women—while they ignore women of color, working-class women, and lesbians.

Talking with Latina, African-American, and white women—including both heterosexual and lesbian women—reveals that the origins of eating problems have little or nothing to do with vanity or obsession with appearance. In fact, eating problems begin as survival strategies—as sensible acts of self-preservation—in response to myriad injustices including racism, sexism, homophobia, classism, the stress of acculturation, and emotional, physical, and sexual abuse. The women I interviewed for this book told me stories that starkly expose how eating problems often begin as an orderly and sane response to insane circumstances.

Their candid stories about how and why they turned to food to cope requires that the reader grapple with the idea of both subtle and overt injustices regularly visited upon women. Some of the experiences the women described are of outrageous, deliberate, and sometimes brutal acts that compromised their ability to feel safe—to be comfortable and sure—in their bodies and in the world. Their experiences reveal both how they developed eating problems and how their ingenious methods of healing are nothing less than testimonies of endurance and empowerment. Their creative strategies for carrying on with their lives—often against great odds—along with their dedication to healing their minds, bodies, and spirits, give yet another face to Minnie Ransom's wise words in Toni Cade Bambara's novel *The Salt Eaters*: "Wholeness is no trifling matter."

On a concrete level, then, the book explains why eating problems are logical, creative responses to trauma, and it identifies effective methods of healing. On a political level, the book posits that bingeing, purging, and starving will continue until women's access to racial, social, sexual, and political justice is ensured. On a more philosophical level, it suggests that women who face injustice have much to teach about faith and resistance, trauma and coping, creativity and despair. My hope is that the book does justice to the experiences of the women I interviewed, reinforcing their ability to—in the words of Richard Wright—"create a sense of the hunger for life that gnaws in us all, to keep alive in our hearts a sense of the inexpressibly human."[2]

Origins of This Book

Embedded in public and medical perceptions of health and disease are metaphors created to explain, engage with, and sometimes dismiss illness. In her creative and expansive approach to scholarship, Susan Sontag has unpacked metaphors surrounding cancer, documenting how cancer has been regarded as a disease of the psychically defeated, the inexpressive, and the repressed. As a cancer patient herself, Sontag was enraged by how much "the very reputation of this illness added to the suffering of those who have it."[3] In her later work, Sontag expanded this framework with her illuminating insights about AIDS, detailing how metaphors about illness reveal much about current states of social disease. She is particularly interested in illness metaphors that, she believes, are used to justify authoritarian rule and militarism. She traces the origins of these militaristic metaphors back to World War I in explanations about syphilis and tuberculosis. These afflictions were described as invasions of alien organisms to which the body responds with its own militaristic operation. While militaristic metaphors still predominate in descriptions about disease, particularly with regard to AIDS, the identity of the enemy has changed. In this shifting use of metaphors, the threat to supremacy is no longer Russia or communism; rather, it is domestic, a result of changing relations in an increasingly multicultural world.[4] In a quintessential social constructionist analysis, Sontag roots conceptions of disease within their historical contexts, capturing public anxiety and political conflicts as they are projected onto human illness.

Like many illnesses represented in the public imagination—such as cancer and AIDS—eating problems are imbued with their own images. Among them is the image of anorexia and bulimia as transitory, self-inflicted obsessions developed by young women lost in their own worlds of fashion and calorie counting. The cost of the dedication to this idea is paid by those with eating problems.[5] While many know that Karen Carpenter's death was caused by anorexia, few are aware that she was only one of about 1,000 women who, according to National Institute of Mental Health estimates, die of anorexia each year. Public knowledge about deaths from eating problems remains scant, partly because deaths linked to them are often labeled differently—as heart or multiple organ failure. While attention to mortality rates can be used to overdramatize eating problems, this information remains an important way to confront one of the most powerful assumptions about eating problems: that although they are prevalent, they are decadent acts of self-obsession that are neither long term nor life threatening.

In 1984 I began to conduct workshops on eating problems among women and men, and, over time, I started to question this vexing portrayal along with the standard profile that has been attached to it. I soon saw that while many women fit the usual profile—white, middle and upper class, heterosexual—many did not. I began to look, largely in vain, for research about women of color and lesbians, and I resorted to incorporating any anecdotal evidence I could find. I cited, for example, Dinah Washington, the jazz singer whose untimely death resulted from a lethal combination of alcohol and diet pills; Oprah Winfrey, whose struggles with her weight have been followed by millions of television viewers; the multigenerational eating problems among African-American women in Gloria Naylor's *Linden Hills*; and poetry about anorexia by the prominent Puerto Rican writer Luz Maria Umpierre-Herrera.[6] My friend Mary Gilfus, a social worker and sociologist who has worked in a women's prison, told me that many incarcerated women are bulimic. Other prison activists have also noted the widespread use of laxatives among women in prison.[7] Prison policy supports the development of eating problems. Healthy food is rarely available; the meals are high in fat and starch, which makes it difficult not to gain weight. Because of severe restrictions on freedom of movement, the act of eating takes on an importance that makes incarcerated women vulnerable to bingeing. The fact that they are disproportionately African-American, Latina, poor, and working-class women raises further questions about the standard profile of women with eating problems.

My interest in women's health in general and my increasing frustration with the dearth of information on eating problems among women of color and lesbians led me to write this book. I conducted eighteen in-depth interviews with African-American, Latina, and white women with eating problems, which allowed me to scrutinize the standard profile and to develop a framework in many ways different from the one offered by the popular media and held by many researchers. Of the women I interviewed, two-thirds have had eating problems for more than half their lives—which counters the popular conception of anorexia and bulimia as transitional and temporary. The fact that the average age among the women I interviewed was thirty-three does not support the common belief that eating problems are primarily teenage problems. Several women were taught to diet, binge, and purge by older relatives—who had done so for years themselves—which suggests that eating problems may not be as historically specific as is typically thought. When eating troubles are seen as survival strategies rather than as responses to strictures about size and shape, they can be identified long before Twiggy's arrival on the fashion scene and Jane Fonda's exercise regimes.

A multiracial focus also raises questions about the adequacy of the theoretical models used to explain eating problems. The biomedical model offers important scientific research about possible physiological causes of eating problems and the physiological dangers of purging and starvation. However, this model adopts medical treatment strategies that may disempower and traumatize women, and it ignores many historical and cultural factors that influence women's eating patterns. The psychological model identifies eating problems as "multidimensional disorders" that are influenced by biological, psychological, and cultural factors. While it is useful in its exploration of effective therapeutic treatments, this model, like the biomedical one, tends to neglect women of color, lesbians, and working-class women.[8]

A third model, offered by feminists, opened up the field of inquiry in crucial ways. With the emergence of feminist work, eating problems were rescued from the realm of individual pathology. When Susie Or-bach's *Fat Is a Feminist Issue* was published in 1978, its critique of dieting and self-denial and its convincing plea for understanding bingeing as a way women cope with living in a society that relegates them to second-class citizenship made it a handbook for thousands of women. This was one of many important books by therapists, sociologists, physicians, and researchers that focused on gender.[9] The fact that most people with eating problems are women was no longer considered simply a factor in but rather integral to understanding anorexia and bulimia.

Feminists argue that patriarchy—which limits women's access to power both within and outside the family—is at the root of women's eating problems. Most women are relegated to sex-segregated jobs that pay them less well than men are paid for comparable work. What is typically referred to as the "glass ceiling" in employment is actually a euphemism for real men's bodies blocking most women's advancement. These barriers, coupled with educational systems that still steer girls away from mathematics, science, and competitive sports, help explain why adolescent girls' self-esteem declines as boys' self-esteem increases. In this context, eating problems signal women's many hungers—for recognition, achievement, and encouragement. It is no surprise that appetites and food take on metaphorical significance in a society in which women typically are responsible for food preparation and yet are taught to deny themselves ample appetites; girls are taught that the barriers they face are their own fault and therefore require individual solutions; and female socialization means caring for others, often at one's own expense.

Rightfully, feminists have raised questions about why the emphasis on dieting and thinness has become so severe. In her groundbreaking book *The Obsession: Reflections on the Tyranny of Slenderness*, Kim Chernin argues that in this historical period of women's increased struggle for economic, legal, and sexual power, one form of patriarchal backlash is defining female beauty as childlike and thin. Chernin writes, "In this age of feminist assertion men are drawn to women of childish body and mind because there is something less disturbing about the vulnerability and helplessness of a small child and something truly disturbing about the body and mind of a mature woman."[10]

In the United States, this image is upheld by interlocking institutional powers: a multi-million-dollar weight-reducing industry in which most of the consumers are women; medical professionals who maintain the dubious assumption that fat is by definition unhealthy and ought to be eliminated; a multi-million-dollar advertising industry that promotes demeaning images of women; a job market in which women who do not fit this model of beauty face discrimination; and an insurance industry that upholds medically prescribed standards of what constitutes a healthy body size. A 1984 national poll of 33,000 women conducted by *Glamour* magazine found that the majority of women surveyed were ashamed of their stomachs, hips, and thighs — parts of the body that contribute to female shapes. The pressure to diet that many girls face from a very young age is an example of an assault aimed directly at the very parts of bodies that are decidedly female — as women throw up and out, excise or diet away breasts, hips, and buttocks.[11] Feminists rightfully ask how different the quality of women's lives might be if the enormous energy they are taught to invest in denying themselves food were redirected toward dismantling sexism in all its many manifestations.

Feminists have also spearheaded research on the connections between eating problems and sexual abuse. In so doing, they have laid the foundation for understanding other traumatic origins of many eating problems. Identifying the functional basis of bingeing and purging helps take eating problems out of the realm of "disorder" and into the realm of coping mechanisms.[12] As is true of feminist frameworks on the field of health in general, feminist research on eating problems has refused to diagnose them as individual psychic conflicts. Portraying them as individual "disorders" rather than as responses to physical and psychological distress is part of a historical tendency to mislabel the results of social injustices as individual pathologies.[13] It is for this reason that some feminist theorists, including me, avoid using the term "disorder" altogether in relation to women's eating patterns, particularly since, for many women, bingeing, purging, and dieting begin as creative coping mechanisms in highly "disordered" circumstances.[14]

Despite significant feminist contributions, scholarship typically has focused on gender to the exclusion of other analytical categories — specifically, race, sexuality, and class. This imbalance in the literature on eating problems mirrors similar exclusionary practices in much white feminist scholarship that bases its theoretical framework on a false universalism.[15] In this way, scholarship on eating problems is not particularly behind in its lack of attention to race, sexuality, and class. Unfortunately, it mirrors health scholarship in general.

This research historically has failed to consider race a significant focus, often treating race or gender or both as "afterthoughts in analyses rather than main points of research studies."[16] Until recently, research on cancer and alcoholism, for example, has paid little attention to African-American women, despite the fact that black women die of cancer far more frequently than white women do.[17] The initial nomenclature for AIDS—gay-related immunodeficiency—identified an "at risk" population that erroneously excluded women and heterosexual men. Although women of color in the United States are now the fastest-growing group infected with the HIV virus, government programs and most private agencies are still poorly equipped to respond to their health care needs.[18]

Rethinking biased assumptions in the literature on eating problems begins with scrutinizing ideas about femininity and gender socialization.[19] For example, the belief that women's bodily insecurities are fueled by lessons about femininity that teach women to be passive and compliant may accurately describe socialization patterns among middle- and upper-class Protestant white women, but this does not apply to many African-American and Jewish women, who are often encouraged to be assertive, self-directed, and active both within their families and publicly. Nor do passivity and dependence accurately describe lesbians and single, divorced, and widowed women who do not rely upon men for economic support and who tend to work in the paid labor market all of their lives. The notion that an institutional imperative toward thinness is a backlash against women's economic gains does speak to the advances of white middle- and upper-class women. But, as these women have been struggling to move up the occupational ladder, working-class women of all races have been striving simply to stay on the ladder—a ladder that, for them, has been horizontally rather than vertically positioned. While women of all classes and races are affected by a backlash Susan Faludi rightfully termed "the undeclared war against American women,"[20] the link some theorists draw between this backlash and augmented economic power is a race- and class-specific supposition that reinforces the association of eating problems with "achievement-oriented" business and professional women. Once again, anorexia and bulimia are rendered invisible among working-class women.

Similarly, the connection drawn between an increase in eating problems and "superwoman" expectations—as more women juggle careers and family responsibilities—accurately identifies changes in the participation of white middle-class women in the paid labor market. More middle-class white women are balancing two full-time jobs, but this double duty is not new for working- and middle-class women of color, lesbians, and single mothers. As white middle-class women have been fighting for the right to work outside the home, many black and Latina women have been fighting for the opposite: a chance to stay home with their children.

Race and class stratification breaks apart a singular reliance upon sexism as the underlying cause of eating problems. The women I interviewed linked the origins of their eating problems to many different types of trauma, many of which have received scant attention from researchers or the media.[21] More than half of them—across race and class—were survivors of sexual abuse, which was often peppered with racism or anti-Semitism. Some women tied eating problems to a range of class factors, including poverty and stress caused by upward class mobility. Among the lesbians, some developed eating problems to cope with homophobia. Other traumas women linked to eating problems were emotional and physical abuse, often laced with racism, and witnessing abuse of siblings or parents.

The multiple traumas women link to their eating problems do not discount the important feminist analyses of the impact of sexist assaults against women's bodies and appetites. A multiracial focus, however, complicates the picture considerably. While feminists have shown how emotional, physical, and sexual abuse may lead women to binge or purge, little attention has been given to how inequalities besides sexist ones change women's eating patterns. Such a focus requires an expanded understanding of trauma that includes not only physical but also psychic injuries. In this way, trauma may include what Harriette McAdoo has termed the "mundane extreme environmental stress" of racism,[22] injuries from poverty, incest and other sexual abuse, physical and emotional abuse, immigration, battery, heterosexism, and a variety of other socially induced injuries.

It is frightening to consider that the many extraordinary and harrowing accounts of trauma the women I interviewed identified may not, in fact, be uncommon. One African-American woman began bingeing when she was four years old because it gave her reliable comfort from the pain of sexual abuse, racism, and witnessing the battering of her mother. A white upper middle class Jewish woman attributed fasting for days on end to sexual and emotional abuse by her boyfriend. Pressed into isolation with the threat of further abuse, this woman began to think she deserved no pleasures—eating, seeing people, or even going out in the sunlight. She locked herself up in her dormitory room, sometimes even in her closet, and starved herself. A Latina woman described her body as a "shock absorber" that attracted the "world's pain," going back as far as she could remember. She ate to buffer herself from this pain. She remembered wondering at the age of five if an entire picnic table of hot dogs, hamburgers, chips, potato salad, and buns would be enough to fill her. Beset by emotional abuse and her relatives' constant criticism of her weight, she had little chance to understand either her body or her appetite as trustworthy or safe.

Identifying the traumatic bases of many eating problems reveals the dangers of labeling a common way women cope with pain as an appearance-based disorder. One blatant example of sexism is the notion that women's foremost worries are about their appearance—a belittling stereotype that masks women's worries about paying the bills, keeping their children off the streets and in school, and building loving and egalitarian relationships. By highlighting the emphasis on slenderness, the dominant imagery about eating problems falls into the same trap of assuming that difficulties with eating reflect women's "obsession" with appearance. This misnaming fails to account for the often creative and ingenious ways that girls and women cope with multiple hardships, quite frequently with no one's help but their own.

The culture-of-thinness model has also been used, erroneously, to dismiss eating problems among women of color based on the notion that they are not interested in or affected by a culture that demands thinness. This ideology lumps into one category a stunning array of racial and ethnic groups—Japanese-Americans, Chicanas, Hopi, Puerto Ricans, Amerasians, and African-Americans, to name just a few. The tremendous cultural, religious, and historical diversity among these groups of people makes the notion that they are—as a whole— invulnerable to eating problems dubious at best.

Emphasis on thinness is certainly not universal or equally tenacious across race and ethnicity. There are aspects of African-American culture, for example, that historically have protected against a demand for very thin bodies.[23] In addition, festivities that take place when food is being prepared and eaten are key aspects of maintaining racial identity. Many black women writers, for example, include positive images of physically large women who enjoy food, and celebrate women of varying shapes and sizes. In fact, Alice Walker's definition of "womanist" includes a woman who "loves love and food and roundness."[24] In her poem "Song for a Thin Sister," Audre Lorde also celebrates size and rejects the notion of thinness as an ideal:

> Either heard or taught
> as girls   we thought
> that skinny was funny
> or a little bit   silly
> and   feeling a pull
> toward the large and the colorful
> I would joke you   when
> you grew too thin.
>
> But your new kind of hunger
> makes me chilly   like danger
> I see you forever retreating
> shrinking   into a stranger

> in flight
> and growing up
> Black   and fat
> I was so sure that   skinny
> was funny   or silly
> but always
> white.[25]

In her poetic voice, Lorde associates "skinny" with whiteness and a culture outside her own. One African-American woman I interviewed was raised in a rural community in Arkansas that valued women of ample proportions. One Puerto Rican woman was given appetite stimulants as a child because her mother thought that skinny children looked sickly.

This ethic did not, however, stop either of them from developing eating problems. In her chronicle about eating problems, Georgiana Arnold, an African-American health educator, identifies dual and conflicting patterns about food. While eating was a joyful part of family life, fat was a topic that the family avoided:

> In our home, food was a source of nourishment, a sign of love, a reward and the heart of family celebrations. It was also a source of ambivalence, guilt, shame, and conflict. Our "family fat" issues descended into the same cavern of silence that housed my father's alcoholism, gambling and willful disappearance from our lives. There was no talking about it and there were no tears.[26]

Ironically, an ethic that celebrates food and protects against internalizing a value of thinness can work against identifying and getting help for eating problems. Furthermore, since there is no such thing as a monolithic "black community," any attempt to identify a single idea about weight, size, and food quickly breaks down.

A multiracial focus does not make the culture of thinness insignificant, but shows that its power needs to be understood in the context of other factors.[27] For some girls, an imperative toward thinness initially has little or nothing to do with their eating problems. They link other social injustices to their eating difficulties. Furthermore, those who do internalize an emphasis on thinness also attribute other injustices to anorexia or bulimia.

By questioning the prominence of the culture-of-thinness model, I do not want to suggest that women avoid talking about their desires to be thin. Issues of appearance are essential currency for women's access to power in this country, and thinness is a critical component. While fat men are vulnerable to ridicule and discrimination, the standards are clearly gendered: being a fat woman is a far graver "mistake" than being a fat man. For white young women, thinness may, in fact, be the most powerful marker used to judge their physical attractiveness. But for women of color, body size is only one of many factors used to judge attractiveness. For older women of any race, the approval of thinness is countered by disdain for wrinkles and an aging body. For lesbians, cashing in on the power of thinness depends upon taking care not to look too "butch."[28] Stereotypes aimed at lesbians of color who are not thin are a stark example of what Barbara Smith termed the "simultaneity of oppression."[29] Nedhera Landers, a black lesbian who is fat, explains:

> My mere existence shows up society's lies in great relief. Being Black (and a chick) would eliminate my being fat. But since I am fat, young and childless, that must mean I'm a whore out of desperation for a man. But, since I am a lesbian and men aren't central to my life, that would eliminate my whore status. So, according to the current myths, I don't exist. When I assert my presence and insist that I am indeed fully present, I become an object of ridicule.[30]

Ultimately, more troubling than what the reliance on the ideal of thinness reveals about health research is what it may signal about U.S. society in general: it speaks to a social inability to openly confront and deal with the results of injustice. In a country brimming with glorified images of youth, whiteness, thinness, and wealth, it makes painful sense that dissatisfaction with appearance often serves as a stand-in for topics that are still invisible.

In fact, it is hard to imagine what the world might be like if people were able to talk about trauma and the ways they cope with it with the same ease as they talk about dissatisfaction with their weight and appearance. The fact that Anita Hill was herself put on trial for testifying about sexual and racial harassment is a glaring indicator that much that we need to know about injustice and people's responses to it is still "unspeakable." The fact that more energy has been spent taking the hateful images of Public Enemy off the music racks—on the premise that the lyrics incite violence—than regulating the guns responsible for the death of thousands of young people is a glaring example of the politics of distraction.[31] The Bush and Reagan administrations' use of the military term "vertical insertion"—a euphemism for the bombing and death of human beings—is a searing example of how language is used to hide violence and violation. In the words of Judith Herman, the "ordinary response to atrocities is to banish them from consciousness. Certain violations of the social contract are too terrible to utter aloud: this is the meaning of the word unspeakable."[32] For a staggering number of women, atrocities done to them have been rendered unspeakable. In the place of this unuttered language are symbolic representations of their traumas—often manifested in unwanted eating patterns and supreme dissatisfaction with appetites and bodies.

Of course, not all women with eating problems have developed them to cope with trauma. The fact that 80 percent of fourth grade girls in one large study said they were on diets and that dissatisfaction with weight and size is in fact normative for women in the United States indicates the danger of such a sweeping generalization.[33] A key distinction between periodic dieting and body disapproval and potentially life-threatening and long-term eating problems may be the history of abuse underlying them. Different exposure to trauma may distinguish a young girl who constantly worries about her weight from a woman for whom bulimia is the centerpiece of her day, a woman who occasionally uses liquid diets from a woman who, at eighty pounds, remains afraid to eat. Explicating possible distinctions like these would require examining trauma in different categories of women. This is a study yet to be done. But the experiences of the women whose lives form the basis of this book reveal that discomfort with weight, bodies, and appetite are often the metaphors girls and women use to speak about atrocities. To hear only concerns about appearance or gender inequality is to miss the complex origins of eating problems.

The Politics of Invisibility

How were women of color and lesbians left out of media attention and research on eating problems in the first place, given that the stereotype of eating problems as a golden girl's disease is probably more indicative of which women have been studied than of actual prevalence?[34] Certainly, the common reliance on studies conducted in hospitals, clinical settings, private high schools, and colleges skewed public perceptions of those most vulnerable to developing anorexia or bulimia.[35] Basing theory on studies restricted to these locations has limited knowledge of women who are not in college, of women of color, of older women and poor women.

This skewed focus has long-term and potentially debilitating consequences. The stereotype that eating problems are "white girl" phenomena has led many highly trained professionals to either misdiagnose or ignore women of color. Maria Root explains that "social stereotypes of plump or obese Black, Latina or American Indian women may avert the therapist from examining any issues around food and body image. Similarly a thin, Japanese American woman may not be assessed for an eating disorder."[36] When women of color are treated, their eating problems tend to be more severe as a result of delays in diagnosis. Among the women I interviewed, only two had been diagnosed bulimic or anorexic by physicians, yet all who said they were anorexic or bulimic fit the diagnostic criteria (DSM-111) for these diagnoses.

Given these realities, a more important question than *how* these groups of women have been made invisible may be *why* theorists and the media have been dedicated to stereotyped images of eating problems.[37] The answer to this question lies in the way that ideology about black women's bodies has been invisibly inscribed onto what is professed about white women's bodies. In her work on biases in higher education curricula, Patricia Hill Collins explains, "While it may appear that the curriculum is 'Black womanless' and that African-American women have been 'excluded,' in actuality subordinated groups have been included in traditional disciplines through the groups' invisibility."[38] Toni Morrison also offers essential tools for uncovering ideology about race and racism in literature, tools that apply well to developing race-conscious health research. In her groundbreaking essay "Unspeakable Things Unspoken: The Afro-American Presence in American Literature"—which she later expanded into the book *Playing in the Dark*—Morrison unravels the illusion that traditional literature in the United States has been "race free" or "universal," recognizing the presence of Afro-Americans, whether spoken or not, in the work of such well-known white writers as Melville, Poe, Hawthorne, Twain, Faulkner, Cather, and Hemingway, to name a few. Using Melville as a case in point, Morrison recognizes the presence of Afro-Americans and slavery in *Moby Dick*, pointing out that traditional American literature is both informed and determined by this presence. For Morrison, this analysis doubles the fascination and power of the great American writers. She warns us that "defending the Eurocentric Western posture in literature as not only 'universal' but also 'race-free' may have resulted in lobotomizing that literature, and in diminishing both the art and the artist."[39] Avoiding future lobotomies, she writes, depends on excavating the "ghost in the machine"—the ways in which the "presence of Afro-Americans has shaped the choices, the language, the structure and the meaning of so much American literature."[40]

Morrison's method of searching for the ghost in the machine of American literature can reveal substantial biases in research on women's mental health. This tool for theoretical excavation dredges up stereotypes of women of color, lesbians, and working-class women that not only are debilitating for these women but also ultimately backfire on white heterosexual women as well.

The portrayal of bulimia and anorexia as appearance-based disorders is rooted in a notion of femininity in which white middle- and upper-class women are presented as frivolous, obsessed with their bodies, and accepting of narrow gender roles. This representation, like the reputation of AIDS and some cancers, fuels people's tremendous shame and guilt about them. The depiction of middle-class women as vain and obsessive is intimately linked to the assumption that working-class women are the opposite: one step away from being hungry, ugly, and therefore not susceptible to eating problems. The dichotomy drawn between working-class and middle-class women reflects the biased notion that middle-class people create symbolic, abstract relations through their actions and thought while working-class people relate to the world in literal, concrete ways. Within this framework, middle- and upper-class women's eating patterns are imbued with all kinds of symbolic significance—as a way of rebelling against parents, striving for perfection, and responding to conflicting gender expectations. The logic that working-class women are exempt from eating problems, by contrast, strips away any possible symbolic significance or emotional sustenance that food may have or give in their lives. Recognizing that women may develop eating problems to cope with poverty challenges the notion that eating problems are class bound and confirms that both middle- and working-class women are quite capable of creating sophisticated and symbolic relations with food that go far beyond a biological need for calories.

Like biased notions about class, the belief that African-American women are somehow untouched by the cult of thinness is built on long-standing dichotomies—good/bad, pretty/ugly, sexually uptight/sexually loose—about white and black women. These divisions feed into an erroneous notion of black women as somehow separate from a society in which beauty standards are an integral part of the socialization of all women. The portrayal of white women as frivolous and obsessed with their appearance is linked to the presentation of black women as the opposite: as unattractive "mammies" who are incapable of being thin or who are not affected by pressures to be thin. With these multiple distortions, the fact that the dress and "look" of black youth have frequently set the standard for what constitutes style in the fashion industry is entirely unaccounted for.

In an autobiographical account, Retha Powers, an African-American woman, describes being told not to worry about her eating problems because "fat is more acceptable in the Black community." Stereotypical perceptions held by her peers and teachers of the "maternal Black woman" and the "persistent mammy-brickhouse Black woman image" added to Powers's difficulty in finding people willing to take her problems with food seriously.[41] The association of eating problems with "whiteness" has made some women of color unwilling to seek help. Getting help may feel like "selling out" or being treated as an oddity by friends or medical professionals.[42] The racist underpinnings of some health care policies historically have also led some women of color to avoid seeking help out of fear of being treated in a prejudicial way. Furthermore, the historical view of black women as bodies without minds underlies their invisibility in the frame of reference; they are dismissed as incapable of developing problems that are both psychological and physical. With the dichotomy drawn between black and white women, Latinas drop out of the frame of reference altogether.

Failing to consider eating problems among lesbians reflects the unwritten but powerful belief that lesbians are not interested in or capable of being "attractive" in the dominant sense of the word. This reflects stereotypical notions of "butches" who are too ugly to care about their weight; women who have "become" lesbians because of fear of men and who have subsequently lost touch with "mainstream" society; and women who settle for women after being rejected by men. As biased notions about race reflect racial fears, so distorted ideas about sexuality reflect fears about sexuality in general, and these fears historically have been projected onto lesbians' bodies. These distortions have not only pushed attention to lesbians with eating problems out of the frame of reference, they have also rendered invisible the many ways lesbian communities have refashioned what constitutes beauty in ways that nurture multiple versions of style, glamour, and grace. It is no coincidence that much of the activism and scholarship opposing "fat oppression" has been spearheaded by lesbian feminists who astutely analyze how discrimination against fat women reflects a society hostile to women who take up space and refuse to put boundaries around their hunger for food, resources, and love.[43]

The notion that eating problems are limited to heterosexual women has also contributed to some lesbians' secrecy. The historical association of lesbian sexuality with mental illness and deviance undercuts many lesbians' willingness to identify themselves with any stigmatizing illness. This institutional bias has been coupled with secrecy among lesbians based on the fear of being misunderstood or rejected by other lesbians. The connotation of anorexia and bulimia as problems developed by those who accept male models of beauty means that a lesbian with an eating problem is admitting to being male-centered and therefore not appropriately lesbian. In this way, linking eating problems with appearance rather than trauma has impeded lesbians' self-diagnosis.

Pioneering research on lesbians has confronted the problematic assumptions underlying their invisibility.[44] Like the emerging research on race, this scholarship links unwanted eating patterns and internalized oppression—the process by which people from subordinated communities accept negative attitudes about themselves that are created by the dominant culture. In addition, although lesbian communities may offer women more generous versions of what constitutes health and beauty, this ethic may not be able to compete with dominant cultural beliefs about body size and weight.[45] The scholarship on lesbians, like that on African-American women, reveals cultural methods of protection against harmful social standards previously missing in research that treated white heterosexual women as the standard.

The intricacies of race, class, and sexuality encourage us to rethink demeaning assumptions about white middle-class femininity and racist assumptions about women of color and to consider bulimia and anorexia serious responses to injustices. At their core, bulimia and anorexia are not signs of self-centered vanity and obsession with appearance but rather, at least in their initial stages, are sensible ways women cope with the difficulties in their lives. Reexamining split and oppositional images about race, class, and sexuality with a wide-angle lens reveals a single complicated frame. A multiracial focus shows that distorted notions about black, Latina, and lesbian women are embedded—both explicitly and implicitly—in notions about white heterosexual women, and that it is impossible to understand any of them without the others.

Body Consciousness

The traumatic basis of many women's eating problems can teach us much about bodies and embodiment, for trauma often disrupts an intact sense of one's body. Women's ways of using food are emblematic of a rupturing of women's embodiment, of their ability to see themselves as grounded in and connected to their bodies.

When I first began to ask women about their relationships to their bodies, I asked them to tell me about their body images, but I soon realized a basic conceptual problem in my question. By inquiring about their body "image" I was taking for granted that they imagined themselves as having bodies, an assumption that many women quickly dispelled. The notion that someone can imagine her body assumes that she considers herself to *have* a body. Some women do not see themselves as having bodies at all.

This painful reality is partly a consequence of oppression that has both historical and contemporary manifestations. The more than three hundred years of slavery in this country robbed African-American men and women of the right to own their own bodies. African-American women were forced into this country as pieces of property "whose purpose was to provide free labor. . . . Their roles in U.S. society were synonymous with work, labor outside of the home, and legitimized sexual victimization from the very outset."[46] In the existential nightmare of slavery, no self was legally recognized, and therefore the body could not exist for the self either. Once slavery was abolished, all that black people had were their bodies. The legal right to own one's body, however, does not in itself ensure that one can claim this right. The legacy of slavery still informs black women's experiences of their bodies in profound ways. The portrayal of black women as mammies (women incapable of being sexual), as Sapphires (women who dominate in the family and in the bedroom), and as Jezebels (sexually promiscuous women who willingly participate in sexual exploitation) reflects the projection of white fantasies and sexuality onto black women's bodies.[47] The idea that white women needed protection was built on seeing black women as their opposite—neither worthy of protection nor wanting to be free of sexual violation.

Debilitating and contradictory stereotypes of Latina women are among the complex and limiting messages against which Latinas have struggled. They have been viewed both as highly sexual, irrationally flamboyant temptresses and as obedient, subservient, fat, and passive—good Catholic mothers. In both their historic and contemporary versions, these stereotypes have long-lasting effects on embodiment and physical presence for Latinas. The existence of these stereotypes does not mean they are inevitably internalized. But what embodiment means for black and Latina women cannot be understood without awareness of the struggle and impact of these stereotypes on self-consciousness.

For many women, responding to social injustices directed at their bodies includes trying to escape what seems like the very location of that pain—their bodies. Pecola, a character in Toni Morrison's *The Bluest Eye*, tries to make her body disappear in response to incest, racism, and poverty:

> Letting herself breathe easy now, Pecola covered her head with the quilt. The sick feeling, which she had tried to prevent by holding in her stomach, came quickly in spite of her precaution. There surged in her the desire to heave, but as always, she knew she would not.
>
> "Please, God," she whispered into the palm of her hand. "Please make me disappear." She squeezed her eyes shut. Little parts of her body faded away. Now slowly, now with a rush. Slowly again. Her fingers went, one by one; then her arms disappeared all the way to

the elbow. Her feet now. Yes, that was good. The legs all at once. It
was hardest above the thighs. She had to be real still and pull. Her
stomach would not go. But finally it, too, went away. Then her chest,
her neck. The face was hard, too. Almost done, almost. Only her
tight, tight eyes were left. They were always left.[48]

Pecola's wish to make her body disappear dramatizes the destructive
intersection of sexual abuse, racism, and poverty as no statistic can.
Trying to disappear is an immediate and logical strategy to escape
what Pecola came to believe caused her pain—her brown eyes and
brown body. Her attempt to slip out and away from the reality of a
world bent on destroying her is a vivid example of how women's embodiment is compromised. People facing these injustices cannot take
for granted such a basic and elemental capacity as being able to reside
comfortably in their bodies. And yet the costs of leaving one's body are
monumental.

Ultimately, I put aside the concept of body image and instead
thought about women's relationships to their bodies as forms of consciousness. Body consciousness is shaped by biological changes common to all women—growth spurts during childhood, puberty, menstruation, menopause, and the aging process—and by the changes of
pregnancy and birthing. People are born with a self-consciousness of
mind and body, with an internal body image, and a "sixth sense"—a
body self-awareness and a sense of mind-body integration.[49] It is
through body consciousness that people can often sense danger, intu-
itively know what to do, and identify how they feel. These elemental
and substantial capacities depend on residing within one's body. Embodiment that allows a person to know where his or her body stops
and another's physical body begins may be at the root of a person's
capacity to know him/herself as simultaneously unique and connected
to the world.

Although everyone is born with a sense of embodiment, experience
of it is not universal. The meanings people ascribe to their bodies and
the social injustices that violate embodiment vary across gender, race,
sexuality, class, religion, and nationality. Unlike the term "image,"
which has a psychological, individual connotation, the etymology of
"consciousness" links an awareness of one's social standing directly to
social conditions. Consciousness, as Karl Marx used the term, links individual people's social realities, opportunities, and perspectives to
class. In a similar way, one's body consciousness is linked to one's race,
gender, and sexuality. This connection more accurately captures wom-
en's complicated relationship to their bodies than is conveyed in the
term "image." Representations of black and Latina women's bodies

and their body consciousness are profoundly different from those of white women. Class stratification also shapes body consciousness. Poverty, for example, can significantly alter a woman's relationship to her body. Being denied the chance to own a car, a house, or even furniture can make a poor woman feel as if her body is all she has left.

Women with eating problems certainly do not have a corner on the market in terms of having difficulty residing comfortably within their bodies. As Emily Martin chronicles in her research on women's reproduction, medical and social processes of birthing, menopause, and puberty in the United States fragment women's embodiment.[50] Feminist theorists on disability offer rich analyses of how disability changes women's embodiment. Discriminatory practices against people with disabilities—including limited access to education, employment, independent living, and sexual freedoms—are typically more restricting than actual physical conditions.[51]

The essential issue may not be *if* women struggle to claim their bodies as their own, but rather the differing ways that embodiment is disrupted. Adrienne Rich writes:

> I know no woman—virgin, mother, lesbian, married, celibate—
> whether she earns her keep as a housewife, a cocktail waitress, or a
> scanner of brain waves—for whom her body is not a fundamental
> problem: its clouded meaning, its fertility, its desire, its so-called
> frigidity, its bloody speech, its silences, its changes and mutilations,
> its rapes and ripenings.[52]

In her poetic way, Rich captures the contradictions and complexities of living in one's body.

To complicate this further, women employ a variety of survival strategies in response to violations of their bodies. The poet Wanda Coleman writes:

> The price Black girls pay for not conforming to white standards of
> beauty is extracted in monumental amounts, breath to death. We
> bend our personalities, and sometimes mutilate our bodies in defense.
> Sometimes that bent is "bad attitude," perhaps accompanied by a
> hair-trigger temper, ready to go off at the mildest slight: neck-
> wobbling, hands to hips, boisterous, hostile, niggerish behavior.[53]

Women may also respond to psychic and physical assaults with silent refusals to engage or show rage. They may run away from home or never leave their apartments. They may flunk out of school or hide behind books. The reasons for these coping strategies are complicated and not easily predicted—just as it is not easy to explain why some women develop eating problems and others do not.

Women with eating problems, however, offer special insights about body consciousness because they respond to trauma in particularly bodily ways. Their stories reveal how bingeing, purging, and dieting can change a woman's embodiment, and they provide vivid examples of what it means for a woman to "leave her body."

Leaving the body is a survival strategy many women use when they see no other alternatives. The sophisticated ways in which the women I talked with describe their experiences of their bodies originate in part in their having had to grapple—seriously and over the long term—with the discomfort of being in their bodies. Their stories reveal the social inequalities that whittle away at a woman's ability to identify her body as her own. They explain what it means to be in exile from one's own body, and why this is common. Their testimonies reveal why sexual abuse and racism can lead a teenager who weighs 110 pounds to see herself as fat and to consider her body the cause of her pain. Their stories also highlight the consequences of drastic weight loss and gain on a woman's sense of her body's shape and size. The average weight fluctuation among the women I talked to was seventy-four pounds. Many of the women's weight changed several times in their lives. Substantial and recurrent weight fluctuation raises complicated and painful questions about what it means to be "embodied" since a woman's possession of a significant portion of her body may be in constant flux.

The women's stories reveal that body consciousness is a highly imaginative and simultaneously concrete ability to see one's self as part of one's body and to draw upon the power generated from this embodiment. It is a concrete reality in that, regardless of one's relation to one's body, breathing, eating, sleeping, and simply being require some consciousness of one's body. But body consciousness occurs at the imaginative and symbolic level as well. In the face of debilitating stereotypes and injustices, women do struggle to claim their bodies as their own. The struggle requires being able to see one's own image of one's body rather than the images projected onto it. Consciousness both takes into account oppressive perceptions of the body and rejects what is debilitating about them.

The women's stories also reveal the often ingenious and creative strategies they develop to counter various assaults, strategies that are at the core of their journey toward self-love and empowerment. Self-love and empowerment are profoundly related to the body. Cornel West writes:

> The issue of self-regard, self-esteem, and self-respect is reflected in bodily form. . . . Toni Morrison would say, "Look you've got to love

yourself not only in the abstract; you've got to love your big lips; you've got to love your flat nose; you've got to love your skin, hands, all the way down."[54]

The women whose experiences form the basis of this book identify their injuries and their resistance with honesty and insight. In so doing, they chronicle their despair and resilience, their depression and fortitude, their ingenuity in taking care of themselves.

Methods and Ethics

Conducting life-history interviews enabled me to hear in women's own words how they interpreted the meaning of and reasons behind their eating patterns: what it feels like to turn to food for comfort, how they come to see their bodies as liabilities, and what resources have most helped them develop sane relationships with food and their bodies. They also explain why food begins as, and often remains, the drug of choice for many girls and women.

I interviewed eighteen women ranging in age from nineteen to forty-six, five of them African-American, five Latina, and eight white. All of the white women and four of the women of color are lesbian. I wanted women of color and lesbians to be at the center of my analysis since we know so little about their eating problems. A third of the women are mothers. Five are Jewish, eight are Catholic, and five are Protestant. Three of them grew up outside the United States. They represent various class backgrounds, in terms of both their families of origin and their own current situations.

The majority of the women had a combination of eating problems (at least two of the following: bulimia, compulsive eating, anorexia, extensive dieting), and the particular types often changed during their lives. The most common problems were bingeing and extensive dieting, although half of the women were also anorexic, bulimic, or both. All had problems that were long-term and serious—for some, even life-threatening. The specific types of eating problems did not correlate with race, class, sexuality, or nationality, although the types of trauma the women associate with their unwanted eating patterns did vary with social position. (There are brief biographical sketches of the women at the end of the book.)

I found women willing to be interviewed by letting people know—where I work, in my neighborhood, in political and community groups—about my study. Some of the women approached me, others I asked. I typically had many conversations with them before the interviews, an important step given the secrecy, vulnerability, and fear that many people feel when they talk about eating problems and the pain underlying them.[55]

The women and I also often discussed the origins and purpose of the study, including my personal and intellectual interest in eating problems. Like many feminist scholars, I believe that a researcher's self-disclosure counters power imbalances; people who consent to talk openly about their lives deserve the right to ask the researcher potentially personal questions as well.[56] Self-disclosure does not eliminate power differences based on race, generation, sexual identity, or class, but our common experiences—as lesbians, as women with eating problems, as neighbors, as antiracist activists, our work-related affiliations—did serve as an initial bridge that made it easier to talk about our differences.[57] One Latina woman asked me why a white and perhaps heterosexual woman was doing research about African-American women, Latinas, and lesbians. I explained that my research emerged from antiracist work and my frustration about the dearth of information on mental and physical health concerns of African-American and Latina women. I also talked about how relying upon friendship networks and alliances at work to find women to interview was partially based on my knowledge that women of color might understandably be skeptical of my background and motivations. Her questions about me and the study also gave us a chance to talk about the complexity of sexual identity—how lesbian identity is not necessarily apparent. This ambiguity parallels the complexity of identification for many light-skinned Latinas (such as herself).

A white woman who is a survivor of sexual abuse was quite hesitant and wanted to be sure that she could stop the interview at any time. Learning that her right as the speaker superseded my rights as the researcher influenced her eventual decision to participate. I also spoke about my own worry, as a survivor of sexual abuse and someone who had a long-term eating problem earlier in my life, about talking about this subject with people I did not know well. In both of these situations, the women's candid questions and our discussion about methods and ethics influenced the tenor of the interview process. These conversations allowed women to talk about their fears and worries about not being understood or having to "start from the beginning all the time" in order for their story to make sense.

Tapping into friendship, work, and community networks was an effective way to find women willing to be interviewed since it allowed them to scrutinize me and the project. Many people of color have had to reckon with false generalizations and distortions put forward by white social workers who have not examined their own understanding of race. People who are willing to talk about private, painful, and power-laden issues deserve to know something about both the research and the researcher.

Clearly, the study was in no way random. I was very specific in terms of race and sexuality about who I was hoping to interview. In addition, I sought women who considered themselves to be in the process of healing, surmising that their understanding of the roots of their eating problems would be greater than that of women whose eating difficulties were at their height. I did not approach the research process as an objective observer, in part because I do not think that, for a study of this kind, "objectivity" is possible or ethical. I came to the interviews with biases: believing that the women were courageous to talk on this subject and already skeptical of the dominant imagery associated with eating problems.

During the interviews I used what Patricia Hill Collins calls "an ethic of care," which she defines as understanding that "personal expressiveness, emotions and empathy are central to the knowledge validation process."[58] I had been conducting workshops on eating problems for several years prior to beginning the book and had been personally immersed in the topic for many years before that. From that experience, I responded to the women's stories in a way that I believe heightened their trust and therefore the integrity of the interviews. Had I approached the interviews as an objective observer, I would have been betraying myself and the women who shared their life stories with me.

Because I interviewed only a few women—who were not randomly selected—generalizations based on their experiences need to be made with caution. My point is not to confirm prevalence or even incidence but rather to examine the meaning of eating problems in these women's lives and what they have to teach us about coping, embodiment, and recovery. At the same time, I do not want to overlook the possibility that their experiences reflect a larger reality. The stakes involved in speaking openly about the traumas underlying many eating problems are high, and much injustice remains underground (only one out of ten incidences of sexual abuse is reported, for example). Perhaps the balance lies in both recognizing what makes each of the women's stories unique and understanding how their experiences reflect common injustices and methods of resistance.

Like many feminist and qualitative researchers, I approached the interviews believing that the people being interviewed, not the researcher, are the experts on their lives, that they know the best chronology, emphasis, and methods of telling about their lives. My task was to remind myself of that when I began to proceed otherwise.[59] In some of the interviews I spoke very little, only infrequently asking for clarification. Other interviews were more like conversations, in which I followed along with questions and comments as the women talked about their lives. The ways the women told their stories mirrored the complex detours, the starts and stops, of their lives.

The multiple and textured meanings of their stories often reflected the ways they lived their lives. People often don't remember or describe their lives in a linear sequence, particularly when they're relating experiences of injustice. Judith Herman explains that people who have survived trauma often tell their stories in a "highly emotional, contradictory, and fragmented manner."[60] In open-ended interviews the women explored subjects from more than one angle, which helped me piece together events and emotions that otherwise were too complicated or confusing for me to follow. Their stories revealed why hesitations, silences, and omissions were understandable and inevitable. Like many qualitative anthropologists and sociologists, I am not sure there is such a thing as a complete story: future experience keeps adding to and revising what the present offers. Partial truths and circuitous narratives of lived experience are often the closest approximation of the whole story available.

Body language—particularly the women's eyes—often helped me know when to move on. Typically, I waited for the woman to talk about a topic so I could use her terms rather than impose my own, so she could decide when it was all right to broach a particular subject. I deliberately did not assume a definition of *eating problem* or *recovery*, and I tried to avoid specific terms until the women used them. Humor often played a key role in their stories; laughter frequently mingled with tears.

Almost all of the interviews took place in the women's homes, which gave me vivid insights into their lives, struggles, and dreams. An African-American woman explained that a key component of her healing was to travel to Egypt "to see the birthplace of black people prior to slavery." Her living room was a shrine: statues of Egyptian gods, portraits of Jesus with brown face and curly hair, candles, stones, and other religious instruments she had collected. Seeing her home gave me an understanding I would otherwise have been unable to grasp. A woman who linked her eating problems to poverty let me into her apartment and then bolted her door with four locks and a long metal police bar that she jammed between between the door and a wall as she explained that her home had been broken into three times. She served me tea with powdered milk crystals, having run out of milk—and money—much earlier in the week. A woman who detailed the psychological abuse she suffered at the hands of her husband was forced to stop talking perhaps a dozen times as her husband came crashing into the house, screaming and yelling, interrupting her despite her pleas for privacy.

One woman explicitly requested that the interview occur outside of her home—a request that taught me a lot about language, culture, and acculturation. This young Dominican woman insisted upon meeting me in my office for the interview, which initially worried me because I associated the office with business, distance, and formality. It turned out that this was her way of seeking rather than avoiding intimacy. She lives with her parents and brothers and has never told any of her relatives about her eating problem. She has no privacy at her house, so it would have been impossible for her to talk there. Also, when she thinks about her eating problem, she thinks about it in English (even though she did not learn English until she was sixteen years old). Because she speaks Spanish at home and English at the university, the university seemed like the natural place to talk about this subject.[61]

I transcribed my tapes of the interviews and gave copies to the women who wanted them. I had further conversations with some of the women in which they clarified ideas and made additions to the transcript. Some women said they were glad to have the transcripts but found it too hard to read them. Many said they felt exhilarated, relieved, satisfied, and glad to have told their life stories, although the costs for some were intense. One woman had a number of painful flashbacks during the interview and later told me she had left her body at some point during the interview; she had to have emergency sessions with her therapist and increase her medication for several days after the interview. Another woman had a hard time emotionally after the interview because she had remembered instances of abuse she had not previously recalled.[62] While these two women's experiences were in the minority, they highlight the courage it takes to speak about eating problems and the traumas that often underlie them. I often felt dazed and exhausted after an interview. Sometimes I had difficulty staying fully "present," which I attributed to the pain in some of the women's stories. My reaction is yet another example of why silence about trauma—and the ways people cope with it—remains and why telling life stories is a risky endeavor.

The women's experiences that are the centerpiece of this book play a central role in each chapter. Chapter 2 examines conditions that may make girls vulnerable to developing eating problems. The women's stories offer essential clues about why many girls grow up distrusting their bodies and their appetites. Lessons they are taught about race, religion, sexuality, and ethnicity are the filters through which they learn about food and eating. Chapters 3 and 4 identify connections between eating problems and several forms of trauma—sexual abuse, racism, heterosexism, poverty, acculturation, and emotional and physical abuse. These chapters show how bingeing, purging, and dieting begin as ways women numb pain and cope with violations of their bodies and how survivors of trauma use food as a logical response to injustices, given the limited alternatives available to them. The lives of the women I interviewed show why we need an expansive understanding of how trauma can be inflicted. Many of the women linked eating problems to physical violations, and others associated them with the psychic invasions of heterosexism, poverty, acculturation, racism, and emotional abuse. Recognizing both psychic and physical invasions avoids the historical tendency to identify the body and mind as somehow disconnected entities.

The concluding chapters examine why food is women's drug of choice, how embodiment is shaped by social inequalities, and the women's healing methods. The women's stories reveal that although eating problems begin as sensible responses to various injustices, they may eventually become liabilities. Healing depends upon making the connection between trauma and eating and understanding how violations distort "body consciousness" and appetites. The healing strategies often entail recovering memories through self-help, community, religious, political, and therapy groups. Finding resources that support women financially, emotionally, and spiritually are also keys to recovery.

2 Childhood Lessons: Culture, Race, Class, and Sexuality

If there is one story that is an integral part of the folklore of growing up female, it is the chronicle of the onset of menstruation. These accounts are often embarrassing—a thirteen-year-old girl has to ask her father to tell her what to do, another is sure that people can tell from her face what is going on in her body—and many, like that of the young teenager who gets a red cake with red candles from her mother to celebrate her first period, are funny. Usually told only in the company of other women, these stories of a rite of passage are often filled with pain, ingenuity, and humor—and sometimes joy.

Equally revealing stories about the development of female identity in the United States spring from lessons girls learn about their body sizes and appetites. Whether they are fat or thin, Latina or Jewish (or both), lesbian or heterosexual, girls are barraged by complicated messages about their bodies, skin, hair, and faces. Not surprisingly, girls who do not fit the standard mold—who look like tomboys, whose skin is dark, who have nappy hair, who are chubby or just plain big, who develop early or develop late—are most aware of negative assessments, and their stories are commonly filled with shame and confusion.

Although there is no single message to girls about weight and food that crosses regional, religious, and cultural lines in the United States, early lessons about weight and appetite often leave indelible marks on their lives. Growing up on a working farm may protect a girl from the pressure to diet, but she may learn elsewhere that a big appetite is not acceptable for girls and women. While being raised in the Dominican Republic may help a young girl value women of all sizes, if she emigrates to the United States, the pressures to assimilate culturally and linguistically may make her especially determined to be thin.

Increasingly, one of the few experiences common to growing girls in the United States is the pressure to diet. This pressure not only reveals strictures about body size, it also telegraphs complicated notions about race, culture, and class. A girl's body may become the battleground where parents and other relatives play out their own anxieties. Just as stories about a first menstruation tell us about a family's social traditions and the extent to which the girl's body is respected within them, lessons about weight and eating habits tell us an enormous amount about culture, race, religion, and gender. It is through these familial and cultural lenses that young girls make judgments about their bodies and their appetites. The nuances in the socialization of girls show why—across race, class, and religion—they may become vulnerable to eating problems and demonstrate how many girls begin to use food to cope with trauma.

Growing up Latina

By the year 2020 the single largest minority group in the United States will be Latino people—including the descendants of people who were in what is now the United States before it was "discovered," people who fled El Salvador and Guatemala in the 1970s and 1980s, Puerto Rican people, and a host of others. Latinos share a history of struggling against colonialism and racism, and they share a common language. Other generalizations are often erroneous.

There is no single Latino ethic about body size and eating patterns. Even to profess that there is a common Puerto Rican expectation about women's body size would conflate significant generational and regional differences.[1] The notion that Latinas as a group are somehow protected from or ignorant of cultural pressure to be thin simply does not hold up in the face of their diversity. Nor can it be said that any particular group of women is isolated from the culture of thinness; the mass media have permeated even the most remote corners of the United States. The pressures of assimilation and racism may make some Latinas especially vulnerable to strictures about weight.

The task, then, is to identify both how ethnic, racial, and socioeconomic heterogeneity among Latinos and Latinas influences their socialization and how these factors may make Latinas susceptible to developing eating problems. One of the Latina women I interviewed, Elsa, was raised by German governesses in an upper-class family in Argentina. Another, Julianna, was cared for by her grandmother in a middle-class family in the Dominican Republic. The other three are Puerto Rican women who grew up in the United States and whose backgrounds ranged from working- to upper-middle-class; among these women, the degree of assimilation varied markedly depending on whether Spanish was their first language, the degree of contact with other Latinas, and the extent to which they identified as Puerto Ricans.

What the Latina women learned about weight and size was influenced by nationality. Julianna, who grew up in a small town in the Dominican Republic, was taught that

> people don't think that fat is bad. You don't undermine fat people. You just don't. . . . The picture of a woman is not a woman who has a perfect body that you see on TV. A woman is beautiful because she is a virgin or because she is dedicated to her husband or because she takes care of her kids; because she works at home and does all the things that her husband and family want her to do. But not because she is skinny or fat.

In the Dominican Republic, female beauty is closely linked to being a good wife and mother and obeying gendered expectations about virginity and monogamy. Thinness is not a necessary criterion for beauty, regardless of a woman's class. By contrast, the Argentinian woman, Elsa, said that a woman's weight was the primary criterion for judging her worth. The diets and exercise her father enforced among his wife and daughters were "oppressive and Nazi-like." But judgments about weight varied with class and degree of urbanization:

> The only people who see being fat as a positive thing in Argentina are the very poor or the very rural people who still consider it a sign of wealth or health. But as soon as people move to the bigger cities and are exposed to the magazines and the media, dieting and figures become incredibly important.

None of the Puerto Rican women I talked with benefited from the acceptance of size that the Dominican woman described. Laura, who lived in Puerto Rico with her family for four years when she was a child, recalls that "Latina women were almost expected to be more overweight. Latin women living in Puerto Rico were not uncomfortable with extra weight. To them it wasn't extra. It wasn't an issue."

This didn't help Laura appreciate her own chunky size because her family's disdain for fat people was much more influential. Her father was British and her mother liked to "hang out with wealthy white women," both factors that impeded Laura's ability to adopt the Puerto Rican community's values.

Another Puerto Rican woman, Vera, who grew up in Chicago, was chunky as a child and learned that the people around her disapproved of her size. Vera remembers painful scenes at school and in clothing stores that taught her she should be embarrassed by her body size. Although she was an amazingly limber and energetic student in her ballet class, her mother took her out of it because Vera wasn't thin enough.

African-American Girls and Community Life

Rosalee grew up in Arkansas in a rural African-American community where, as she described it, "home grown and healthy" was the norm. She remembers that her uncles and other men liked a "healthy woman": as they used to say, "They didn't want a neck bone. They liked a picnic ham." Among the people in her community, skin color and hair were more important than weight in determining beauty. Unlike most of the other women I interviewed, Rosalee didn't think about dieting as a way to lose weight until she was a teenager. Because her family didn't always have money, "there were times when we hardly had food anyway so we tended to slim down. And then . . . when the money was rolling in . . . we celebrated. We ate and ate and ate." When poverty is a constant threat, Rosalee explained, "dieting just isn't a household word." This did not stop Rosalee from developing an eating problem when she was four years old as a response to sexual abuse and being a witness to beatings. Trauma, not size, was the primary factor.

Carolyn, a middle-class woman who grew up in an urban area, remembered that her African-American friends considered African-American women of varying weights to be desirable and beautiful. By contrast, among white people she knew, the only women who were considered pretty were petite. Both the white and the African-American men preferred white girls who were petite.

The women who went to schools in which there were only a few African-American students remember thinness as dominant. By contrast, those who went to racially mixed or predominantly African-American schools saw more acceptance of both big and thin women. One of the many hazards for black students who attend overwhelmingly white schools is pressure to adopt cultural values—including thinness—that may not reflect African-American values.[2]

The women who attended private, predominantly white schools were sent by parents who hoped to open up opportunities unavailable in public schools. As a consequence, both Nicole and Joselyn were isolated from other African-American children. Their parents discouraged them from socializing with neighborhood African-American children, who in turn labeled them arrogant, thus furthering their isolation. Both were teased by neighborhood children for being chubby and light-skinned. At school they were teased for being fat and were excluded by white people in ways both subtle and overt. Racist administrators and teachers granted the girls neither the attention nor the dignity they deserved. Joselyn, who attended Catholic schools, remembered both racial and religious intolerance: "Sister Margaret Anna told me that, basically, what a black person could aspire to at that time was to Christianize the cannibals in Africa." Neither Nicole nor Joselyn had a public context in which her racial identity was validated. As Nicole said, "By second or third grade I was saying I wished I was white because kids at school made fun of me. I remember . . . getting on the bus and a kid called me a brown cow." As the women were growing up, their weight and their race were used to ostracize them.

Intersection of Race and Class

Most of the African-American and Latina women were pressured to be thin by at least one and often all of their family members. For some, these pressures were particularly virulent because they were laced with racism. Rosalee, who grew up on a farm in the South, got contradictory messages about weight and size from her family. Like most of the African-Americans in her community, Rosalee's mother thought thin women were sickly and took her young daughters to the doctor because they weren't gaining enough weight. But her father told her she "had better not turn out fat like her mother." Rosalee and her mother often bore the brunt of his disdain as he routinely told them that African-American women were usually fatter and less beautiful than white women. Rosalee says:

> I can remember fantasizing that "I wish I was white." . . . It seemed
> to be the thing to be if you were going to be anything. You know,
> [white women] were considered beautiful. That was reinforced a lot
> by my father, who happened to have a strong liking for white
> women. Once he left the South and he got in the army and traveled
> around and had more freedom, he became very fond of them. In fact,
> he is married to one now. He just went really overboard. I found
> myself wanting to be like that.

Although she was not familiar with dieting as a child, she feared weight gain and her father's judgments. At puberty, she began to diet. Her father's sexism and prejudice against black women meant that she was raised with contradictory messages about weight. At the same time, she was learning about the dominant standard of beauty that emphasizes a fair complexion, blue eyes, and straight hair. About the lessons many black girls learn about straightening their hair and using lightening creams, Rosalee says:

> It was almost as if you were chasing after an impossible dream. I can remember stories about parents pinching their children's noses so they don't get too big. I laugh about it when I am talking about it with other people but on the inside I don't laugh at all. There is nothing there to reinforce who you are, and the body image gets really confused.

Some of the Latinas' and African-Americans' relatives projected their own frustrations and racial prejudices onto the girls' bodies. Joselyn, an African-American woman, remembers her white grandmother telling her she would never be as pretty as her cousins because they had lighter skin. Her grandmother often humiliated Joselyn in front of others, making fun of Joselyn's body while she was naked and telling her she was fat. As a young child Joselyn began to think that although she couldn't change her skin color, she could at least try to be thin.

When Joselyn was young, her grandmother was the only family member who objected to her weight. Then her father also began to encourage his wife and daughter to be thin as the family's social status began to change. When Joselyn was very young, her family was what she called "aspiring to be middle class." For people of Joselyn's parents' generation, having chubby, healthy children was a sign the family was doing well. But, as the family moved up the social ladder, Joselyn's father began to insist that Joselyn be thin:

> When my father's business began to bloom and my father was interacting more with white businessmen and seeing how they did business, suddenly thin became important. If you were a truly well-to-do family, then your family was slim and elegant.

Her grandmother's racism and her father's determined fight to be middle class converged, and Joselyn's body became the playing field for their conflicts. While Joselyn was pressured to diet, her father still served her large portions and bought treats for her and the neighborhood children. These contradictory messages confused her. Like many girls, Joselyn was told she was fat from the time she was very young, even though she wasn't. And, like many of the women I interviewed, Joselyn was put on diet pills and diets before puberty, beginning a cycle of dieting, compulsive eating, and bulimia. She remembers her father telling her, "You know you have a cute face, but from the body down, you are shot to hell. You are built just like your old lady."

Another African-American woman also linked contradictory messages about food to her parents' internalized racism. As Nicole explains it, her mother operated under the "house-nigger mentality," in which she saw herself and her family as separate from and better than other African-American people. Her father shared this attitude, saying that being Cherokee made him different. Her parents sent Nicole to private schools and a "very white Anglican upper-class church" in which she was one of a few black children. According to Nicole, both parents "passed on their internalized racism in terms of judgments around hair or skin color or how a person talks or what is correct or proper."

Their commandments about food and body size were played out on Nicole's body in powerful ways. Nicole's father was from a working-class rural Southern family. Her mother, by contrast, was from a "petit bourgeois family," only one of three black families in a small New Hampshire town. While Nicole's father approved of her being, as he said, "solid," her mother restricted her eating to ensure that Nicole would grow up thin. Each meal, however, was a multicourse event. Like Joselyn, Nicole was taught that eating a lot was a dangerous but integral part of the family tradition:

> When I was growing up, I thought that breakfast was a four- or five-course meal the way you might think dinner is. I thought that breakfast involved fruit and maybe even juice and cereal and then the main course of breakfast, which was eggs and bacon and toast. On Sundays we had fancy breakfasts like fish and hominy grits and corn bread and muffins. So breakfast had at least three courses. That is how we ate. Dinner was mostly meat and potatoes and vegetables and bread. Then my father would cajole my mother into making dessert. There were lots of rewards that all had to do with food, like going to Howard Johnson or Dunkin' Donuts.

At the same time, Nicole's mother put her on a diet when she was three and tortured her about her weight. Nicole became terrified of going to the doctor because she was weighed and lectured about her weight. Yet, after each appointment, her mother took her to Dunkin' Donuts for a powdered jelly doughnut. When her father did the grocery shopping, he bought Nicole treats, which her mother snatched and hid, accusing her father of trying to make her fat. When she was left alone,

Nicole spent hours trying to find the food. In her mother's view, Nicole's weight and curly hair were what kept her from being perfect: her body became the contested territory onto which her parents' pain was projected.

The confusion about body size and class expectations that troubled some of the African-American women paralleled the experiences of two Puerto Rican women. Vera attributed her eating problems partly to the stress of assimilation as her family moved from poverty to the working class. When Vera was three, she was so thin that her mother took her to a doctor who prescribed appetite stimulants. By the time she was eight, though, she remembered her mother comparing her to other girls who stayed on diets or were thin. Vera attributed her mother's change of heart to pressure from family members:

> Even though our family went from poverty to working class, there were members of my extended family who thought they were better than everyone else. As I grew up, the conversation was, "Who is going to college? Who has a job working for Diamonds?" It was always this one-upmanship about who was making it better than who. The one-upmanship centered on being white, being successful, being middle class . . . and it was always, "Ay, Bendito [Oh, God]! She is so fat! What happened?"

Vera's mother warned her that she would never make friends if she was fat. Her mother threatened to get a lock for the refrigerator door and left notes on it reminding Vera not to eat. While Vera's mother shamed her into dieting, she also felt ambivalent when Vera did not eat much. When Vera dieted, her mother would say, "You have to eat. You have to eat something. You can't starve yourself." The messages were always unclear.

Ruthie also remembers changes in the family ethic about size and eating that she attributes to assimilation with Anglo culture. In keeping with Puerto Rican tradition, Ruthie's mother considered chubby children a sign of health and well-being. According to Puerto Rican culture, Ruthie says, "if you are skinny, you are dying. What is wrong with you?" When Ruthie was ten to twelve years old, her mother made her take a food supplement and iron pills that were supposed to make her hungry. Ruthie did not like the supplement and felt fine about the size of her body. But how Ruthie looked was very important to her mother: "My mother used to get these dresses from Spain. She used to show everyone our closets. They were impeccable. Buster Brown shoes and dresses. She thought if I were skinny it would reflect badly on her." Ruthie questioned whether her mother cared about Ruthie or was actually worried about what the family and neighbors would say.

When Ruthie became a teenager, her mother's attitude about weight changed:

> When I was little, it was not okay to be skinny. But then, at a certain
> age, it was not okay to be fat. She would say, "Your sister would
> look great in a bikini and you wouldn't." I thought maybe this was
> because I felt fat. . . . Being thin had become something she valued. It
> was a roller coaster.

Ruthie attributed this change to her mother's acceptance of Anglo standards, which she tried to enforce on Ruthie's eating and body size.

The women's experiences dispel the notion that African-American and Latina women—as a group—are less exposed to or influenced by a culturally imposed thinness than white women. The African-American women who saw community acceptance of different sizes did not escape pressure to be thin from family members. While growing up in a rural area and attending predominantly black schools did protect two of the girls from pressures to diet, childhood traumas resulted in eating problems. For the women of color whose parents' internalized racism, an emphasis on thinness was particularly intense. Rosalee explains:

> For a black woman dealing with issues of self-esteem, if you don't get
> it from your family, you [are punished] twice because you don't get
> self-esteem from society either. If you come from a dysfunctional or
> abusive family, there [are] just not a lot of places to go that will turn
> things around for you.

This reality underscores why some women of color may be more, rather than less, vulnerable than white women to eating problems.

White Girls in Their Families and Communities

As is true of the women of color, ethnic, religious, and national diversity among white women makes it difficult to generalize about a monolithic socialization process. With the exception of a Sephardic Jewish woman who grew up outside the United States, none of the white women I talked with escaped pressure to diet and be thin. Ethnic and religious identity, however, did influence their eating patterns and their attitudes about their bodies. Anti-Semitism and ethnic prejudice shaped the way some of the girls interpreted strictures about weight and eating. Like most of the women of color, the white women had little access to communities in which women of different sizes were valued. Messages that white girls received both in their homes and in their communities promoted dieting and thinness.

All of the American Jewish women I interviewed were taught that they needed to be thin. Although none were fat as children, all had parents who were afraid they would become fat and took what they saw as precautions. One family bought only enough food for one day at a time, reasoning that they would not overeat if no "extra" food was available. Two Jewish women who went to predominantly Protestant schools said belonging to a religious minority exacerbated pressures about body size. Both felt like outsiders because they were Jewish, and their Protestant classmates perceived them as talking, dressing, and looking different.

As for many of the Latinas and African-American women, the discrimination Jewish children experienced was most overt when they were in the minority. Sarah learned that some of her Protestant classmates thought that Jewish people had horns. Both Sarah and Gilda were called names and excluded from friendship groups. Gilda, who is a Sephardic Jew, remembers that when she began to attend school in the United States, other children spit on her and called her "kike":

> It was the craziest thing I have ever experienced. I hadn't experienced it from people I was told we were at war with [in North Africa]. If anything, the Arab women and mothers were more supportive. They would take us in.[3]

Children in the United States called her father the "Tasmanian devil" and made fun of her accent. The Jewish girls coped with discrimination by minimizing the ways they felt different from or inferior to others, including trying to hide their body sizes. Sarah explained that "in the school I attended, where I was only one of a handful of Jewish kids, I never felt like I fit in. I didn't have the right clothes, I didn't look the right way. I didn't come from the right family." When she was as young as eleven, Sarah began to feel "that I had to lose weight or that something wasn't right." Although she wasn't fat, in her mind, she was.

Of the five Jewish women, Gilda—who grew up in North Africa and France before settling in the United States—was the only one exposed to a wholehearted acceptance of food. For Gilda's father, who was raised in North Africa, family meals were a central, celebrated aspect of maintaining North African and Jewish culture:

> First of all food and Friday night and Shabbes. Friday night for my father is a very important time. . . . We have a traditional [North African] meal with vegetables and different salads and [North African] spices. The whole flavor, the whole mood of the evening is not American at all. On holidays, Passover, we read the Haggadah in

French, Arabic, Hebrew, and English. By page thirty, you are ready to die of hunger and exhaustion.

Eating together as a family was an important aspect of this tradition. Although Gilda learned that being a very thin child was not acceptable and that eating was a primary way her father celebrated his culture and religion, she remembered her mother always being on a diet, even though she was never more than slightly overweight. Gilda's father became angry with her when, as an adolescent, Gilda refused to eat with the family and did not keep kosher meals. Contradictory messages from her father and mother and differences between North African and U.S. standards caused confusion about weight and size.

The white women who were raised in Christian families were taught that being thin was crucial for females. Dawn, a middle-class white woman raised in a strict Catholic family, was taught from a young age that "a woman's worth was in her size." Antonia's ideas about eating and weight were deeply affected by her Italian-American ethnic identity. Like some of the Jewish women and women of color, Antonia felt like an outsider at school from kindergarten on, a feeling that was compounded by thinking she was overweight. At school she learned that to be accepted socially, she had to look and act like the "WASPs"—to have straight blond hair and be passive and quiet. She remembers that "I used to get called loud. I talked a lot. Very active. And I was very aggressive. I used to wrestle with the boys a lot. I stood out from other people." Because she was fat, she was often humiliated by other children at school. One of the boys called her "taters" (a big potato). At a high school prom fund-raiser—a "slave auction," where girls were auctioned off—"when it was my turn, no one was bidding. To this day, . . . I can't even really remember the actual sequence of events. It was just the most humiliating thing in my life." When Antonia was eleven, her mother put her on a diet and a doctor prescribed amphetamines. During adolescence she tried to diet but her heart was not in it. In her mind, no amount of dieting would take away her assertive, emotional, and athletic ways, so what was the point in trying to lose weight anyway?

Grooming Girls to Be Heterosexual

While messages to girls about their bodies and appetites are shaped by race, class, ethnicity, and religion, no such diversity exists when it comes to learning about heterosexuality. In both subtle and overt ways, girls—across race, class, ethnicity, and religion—learn that being heterosexual is natural and inevitable. These expectations add up

to what poet and writer Adrienne Rich has termed "compulsory heterosexuality": a largely invisible but enormously powerful force that
orchestrates the range of what is considered acceptable female sexuality.[4] Elements of this enforced heterosexuality include pressure to
marry and have children, male control of female sexuality, and an economic system that makes it difficult for many women to support themselves without marrying—plus prejudice and discrimination against
gay men and lesbians and limitations on how emotionally close people
of the same gender can be without facing reprisals. As girls reach their
teenage years, they are punished if their friendships with other girls become intimate. They are also expected to show an interest in the opposite sex.[5] As Johnnetta Cole writes, women in the United States are
"being measured against an objectified notion of female sexuality
which is eternally young, never fat but 'well developed,' heterosexual,
submissive to 'her man,' and capable of satisfying him sexually. It is
striking how this ideal image cuts across racial, ethnic and class
lines."[6]

The idea that heterosexuality is a necessary condition of "normal
development" is often not overt or explicit unless girls begin to show
signs of not being sufficiently heterosexual. For example, a Puerto Rican lesbian told me:

> My mother would say, there is nothing you can't do, if you want. But
> yet, in other subtle ways, she would encourage me to be a nurse. She
> wouldn't come right out and say, you can't be a doctor. She'd say I
> was supposed to be ladylike.

Being ladylike and having a traditionally female career was a prerequisite for marriage. Being thin was also integral to this heterosexual
expectation.

All of the women I interviewed were taught that heterosexuality
was essential. Many traced strictures about their bodies and appetites
partly to this imperative. Implicit messages were commonly conveyed
in the form of how girls were expected to look, how they were permitted to use their bodies athletically, how they should dress, and how
much they were allowed to eat. For many girls, these rules were most
fiercely applied as they approached puberty. Tomboys who grew up
riding bicycles, playing handball, and wrestling with boys were often
summarily reprimanded as they approached puberty. As they were informed that they should start wearing dresses and go to the junior high
dances, they were also encouraged to "eat like a lady" and pass up second helpings. In some families, boys were allowed to eat all they
wanted while girls were not. The rationale for this double standard
was that girls should be smaller than boys in order to be attractive to

the opposite sex. Some girls remembered hating these restrictions. They missed being physically active, and they resented having to get by with less food.

As they approached their teen years, many were taught that having boyfriends depended upon being thin. One African-American woman remembers initiating her first self-imposed diet because her boyfriend liked thin women. All of his sisters encouraged it, too. When an Argentinean woman was eleven years old her mother told her, "You should really make an effort and diet. You won't be popular around the boys. You are going to have trouble finding a husband. You look terrible. What a pity. You have a nice face but look at your figure." Laura, a Puerto Rican woman, remembers her mother and father both teaching her that she needed to lose weight or run the risk of being an "old maid." Integral to her socialization was the message that being successful heterosexually depended upon being thin:

> One day when I was eleven my parents and I were sitting on the beach in Puerto Rico. There was this blond woman walking down the beach with about ten men around her. She was in a bikini and my father and mother said, "She is not very attractive but she is thin. Look at all those men around her." They pointed out this other woman, who was heavy. She was by herself. She had a very beautiful face. They said, "See, she is beautiful. But she is not thin. She is by herself." It was right out front. That began at eleven years old. You are worthless unless you are thin.

The lessons about heterosexuality often went hand in hand with lessons about weight and dieting. Not surprisingly, those who questioned their heterosexuality at a young age were often best able to identify how these strictures reinforced each other. One of the characteristics of dominant ideology—including compulsory heterosexuality—is that it is understood as significant only when it is transgressed. This is also the power of dominant ideology, since it is often consciously felt only by those who contest it, who are encouraged—and sometimes forced—to accept it. For example, one woman who was not interested in boys during high school and had crushes on girls remembers that the "in group" of girls at school constantly talked about their boyfriends, diets, and losing weight. She partly wanted to be like them and thought that dieting would make her feel included in their friendship circle. Another woman's grandmother and mother taught her that "if you were thin, then all of your problems should be erased. You could be happily married, you could satisfy a man, anything you wanted could be yours if only you could be thin."

None of the girls grew up in homes where heterosexuality was questioned. This taken-for-granted aspect of their socialization meant that all the models for sexuality pivoted on attracting men; there were no alternatives. Consequently, there was no room for the idea that women's appetites and body sizes could be defined according to their own standards rather than norms based on rigid definitions of masculinity and femininity.

Whose Body Is This, Anyway?

Given the complex and sometimes contradictory messages that girls get as they are growing up, it is no wonder that many come of age distrusting their appetites and their bodies. The process highlights many feminist assertions about eating problems, and understanding the impact of gender discrimination takes us a long way toward seeing that many girls must reckon with the question, Whose body is this, anyway?

Girls are bombarded with complicated ideas about their bodies not just within their families; pressures in their communities, schools, and churches also play a vital role. Feminists rightfully recognize that it is impossible to understand girls' attitudes toward their bodies without scrutinizing what goes on both inside and outside their families. This comprehensive scope is especially important for a multiracial focus, since some women of color may get contradictory messages in their communities and in their homes.

Taking community pressures into consideration also counters the psychoanalytic tendency to reduce eating problems to psychic problems caused by mother-daughter dynamics. The psychoanalytic notion that a girl's anorexia is a "reaction to a hostile mother" or a manifestation of a child's unconscious ambivalence toward her mother is problematic when it is seen through a feminist, sociocultural lens.[7] Rather than placing blame solely on mothers, feminists explain that anorexia may be a girl's logical solution to a world in which women's bodies are treated like objects and ridiculed. While nonfeminist theorists may root a girl's anorexia in unconscious conflicts with her mother, feminists argue that it is necessary to look at the entire family. Mothers are not the only ones implicated in encouraging girls to diet and distrust their appetites: fathers, siblings, and other relatives are often responsible as well. Fathers may ridicule girls as their bodies develop, tell them that they should not be "fat like their mother," demand that they diet, and link weight loss to the family's social success.

Whether they're African-American, Latina, or white, most girls grow up learning that being thin is valued—especially for women. All of the women I interviewed talked about being aware of this pressure at some point in their lives. They all experienced the physiological and psychological stress of dieting—which researchers have implicated in the onset of bulimia and anorexia.[8] Family pressure to curb their appetites, use diet pills, and diet did render many vulnerable to anorexia and bulimia. Many of the women were put on diets or were given diet pills before adolescence—perhaps disrupting their metabolisms and making it more rather than less difficult to lose weight. (We now know that persistent dieting can lower the resting metabolism, which can result in weight gain rather than loss.)[9] Diet pills also jeopardize physical strength and sleeping patterns. One woman had routinely cleaned her room in the middle of the night, not knowing that her insomnia was linked to the mescaline in her diet pills. It wasn't until she was in college and saw friends' frenetic activity when they were taking speed that she realized that her childhood hyperactivity was drug-induced. Another woman collapsed and had a seizure in reaction to diet pills. She was rushed to the hospital and prescribed a strong depressant. She remembers being "totally freaked out. I was shaking. I couldn't talk. It was like my tongue had swollen in my mouth and I was completely stoned. . . . That was . . . my first introduction to dieting." A third woman remembers feeling like she was going to pass out playing softball and running track because she had so little food in her body.

Many of the women responded to enforced dieting by sneaking or stealing food and then bingeing secretly. The woman who was hospitalized came home, ate an enormous amount of chicken, and slept for twenty-four hours because she hadn't slept in three weeks. The woman who worried about fainting at sports practice binged as a way of compensating for being deprived of food. Some of the women stole money from their mothers' purses to buy food when they were as young as six and seven. In response to constant teasing about her weight, one woman remembers thinking, "I will show you. I can be as fat as I want. I will still have friends. I would go eat. Stuff myself. I would go get candy. Steal candy. Candy bars. Hide them in my pocket."

Many of the women say that they lost weight but eventually gained back more than they had lost. The presentation of dieting as an inevitable requirement of growing up female initiated a cycle of dieting, bingeing, and purging that, once it was begun, was hard to stop. Enforced dieting undermines a girl's bodily integrity—her ability to control what goes in and out of her body—by making it difficult for her to control her desire to binge. It whittles away her sense of being able to control how much or when she eats, which compromises her belief that she is in charge of her body.

Many of the women had a difficult time developing an accurate sense of their body size and shape as a result of their families' inaccurate and inconsistent assessments. Many who were put on diets would be considered "normal" according to insurance charts. Often what was identified as fat was actually their developing breasts and hips — suggesting that the psychoanalytic assumption that a girl develops eating problems as a result of her own fear of having an adult female body is in at least some cases unwarranted. In fact, others' fears of girls' growing bodies can serve as the catalyst for dieting and disruption of their normal processes of development.

Because the development of hips and breasts was misnamed as fat, the women often lost a realistic sense of their body sizes and shapes. Dawn says, "At age eleven or twelve, when I started to develop, I remember being fascinated. Loving my body. Standing in front of the mirror and looking. Posing with no clothes on. Loving the shape of my waist." During the same year, Dawn remembers, her mother turned to her and said, "You have to be careful. You are starting to put on weight"; "I don't even think I weighed 105 pounds," says Dawn now. In response to this warning,

> I started to realize that actually my hips were a little bigger than they should be. I had already been concerned around food because my sister has always been a little overweight. I got messages from very, very young that a woman's worth is in [her] size.

Stories of parents' confusing observations about their daughters' weight are common. Another woman, Vera, says:

> I was not a fat child. My mother had me believe I was. But I wasn't. I used to look at other girls and compare myself to them. I would think, I am not as thin as her, but I am not as fat as her.

As she tried to develop a realistic understanding of her body's contours, her mother continued to confuse her. Her mother told her that she was so fat she would have to wear a nurse's uniform to her eighth-grade graduation because a uniform store was the only place where they made white clothes big enough for her. The comment devastated her. Actually, though, her mother had already sent for a beautiful dress from Mexico — a size nine, certainly not large for a thirteen-year-old girl who had already been through puberty. She also remembers, when she was fifteen, walking down the street with her mother, who pointed to a woman who weighed 300 pounds:

> When she walked her behind went boom-boom-boom-boom. She was an incredibly obese person. My mother said, "You look just like her.

Your body is exactly like hers." I can remember going home and
standing in front of the mirror and looking and looking and looking.
In my mind I was totally warped as to what I looked like. I was
probably wearing [a size] eleven or thirteen. When I would lose a
little weight I would wear a nine.

Another woman was told by all of her sisters and her mother that she
was the fattest one of them all. She was the last to be served at each
meal and was picked on for being overweight. She cried her way
through most meals. It wasn't until she was an adult that she realized
by looking at pictures that she was not a fat child and that, in fact, her
mother was obese.

Dieting was the initial way many of the women had tried to cope
with confusion about their body sizes. If they were not able to figure
out if they were fat, many reasoned that it wouldn't hurt to diet. Paying close attention to their eating began as an attempt to assert some
control over their bodies. At least initially, this helped avoid being
teased about an "unacceptable" body size and allowed them to coun-
teract what they were being blamed for.

Dieting often backfired. What began as a way to control eating frequently resulted in bingeing and, in some cases, purging. Other traumas exacerbated these cycles. Many of the women have had to adjust
to major changes in their body sizes at least once and often many times
during their lives. Extreme weight fluctuation not only can cause physical damage but also impairs a woman's ability to know her actual
size. Sudden weight gain and loss leaves a woman little time to adjust
to changes in her body dimensions.

American Dreams and Unsatisfied Hungers

The childhood lessons that African-American, Latina, and white
women learn illuminate pressures about body size and appetites that
have not yet been examined in research or focused on by the media.
Jewish and black parents may assume that although they cannot protect their daughters from anti-Semitism and racism, encouraging thinness at least shields them from discrimination against fat people. An
African-American or Latino parent who tells a child not to eat and
then feeds her confuses the child as she learns to feed herself, yet the
feeding may also indicate a cultural tradition of nurturing through
food. When a Puerto Rican mother gives her five-year-old daughter a
food supplement to make her gain weight, then ridicules her when she
gains weight as an adolescent, pressures of assimilation may account
for the mother's change of heart.

To understand why a girl's relatives want her to be thin, we need to know what forms of economic, racial, ethnic, and religious discrimination they have encountered. Underlying an attempt to make a girl thin is an often unspoken assumption that while the family might not be financially stable, or it cannot fully shield her from racism, or it does not speak English without an accent, her small size may make her life and theirs somewhat easier. Some African-American women and Latinas I interviewed related pressure to be thin to their parents' hopes to be middle class, and middle-class standing depended upon upholding this aesthetic. The dual strain of changing class expectations and racism may explain why some of the women of color linked an emphasis on thinness to class pressures while the white women did not. Class does not, by itself, determine whether or not the women were expected to be thin. Supposing that it does implies that poor women — both women of color and white women — are somehow culturally "out of the loop," an assumption that is both demeaning and inaccurate. But changes in class did fuel some parents' desire to control their daughters' appetites.

Pressures on parents do not justify their attempts to mold their daughters' bodies, but understanding why women across race and class develop eating problems requires clarifying what constitutes the "culture" in the culture-of-thinness model. Many people accept the notion that body size is, in fact, something that can be controlled, given enough self-discipline. This ideology makes dieting appear to be a logical strategy. When caretakers demand that their daughters be thin, some may do so believing that they have more control over weight than over other more complex and insidious forces that they have little power to change.

Doing justice to the social context in which eating problems arise also explains why the culture-of-thinness model needs to be considered along with other destructive social forces. Although thinness is an institutionally supported criterion for beauty, imperatives about age, color, and sexuality matter as well. An often-cited 1980 study documents the emergence of the culture of thinness by showing a marked decrease in the weight of centerfold models in *Playboy* magazine and the winners of the Miss America Pageant between 1959 and 1978.[10] This study quantifies a relationship between the social emphasis on thinness and the increase in eating problems but does not point out that, until recently, women in *Playboy* and the Miss America Pageant have been almost exclusively white, young, and heterosexual. Although the study shows that both the magazine and the pageant support a tyranny of slenderness, an integrated analysis would also elucidate tyranny based on the glorification of whiteness, youth, heterosexuality, and able-bodiedness. An expansive understanding of socialization requires scrutiny of the power of racism and classism as they inform standards of appearance. While white skin will not protect a fat woman from weight discrimination, it does protect her from racial discrimination. The resilience of the stereotype of the fat black "mammy" shows the futility and damage of considering standards of beauty as simply gendered. Interpreting socialization inclusively shows the myriad pressures affecting girls' opinions of their bodies. This approach also paves the way for seeing why girls—across race, class, religion, and ethnicity—may turn to food as a reaction to injustice.

3 Ashes Thrown up in the Air

Childhood sexual abuse is a devastating crime that is capable of forever changing children's relationships to their bodies and the world. Nearly 8 million adults in the United States—more than the population of the entire state of New Jersey—were sexually abused as children.[1] At least one out of four girls and one out of seven boys are sexually abused, most often by a man they know and trust.[2] Although public awareness of sexual abuse has increased in the past ten years— largely as a consequence of feminist organizing and the courage of thousands of survivors—common perceptions of the ways survivors "cope" are too often based on reports of sex offenders who have been sexually abused, day-care workers who abuse children and turn out to have been abused themselves, and people who, as a consequence of being violated, are forever unable to live full lives. Rarely do we hear the less sensational stories of people whose methods of coping are so commonplace that they are easily ignored.

Until the mid-1980s, there was little attention to the relationship between sexual abuse and eating problems.[3] This sparse consideration is noteworthy because women with eating problems are frequently survivors of abuse, and both abuse and eating problems significantly disrupt a woman's ability to see her body as her own. In recent years, feminists have confronted the political and theoretical impediments to research on eating problems and sexual abuse, and their inquiry has rendered obsolete and morally bankrupt previous obfuscations of the connection between the two. Many studies confirm that between one-third and two-thirds of women who have eating problems have been sexually abused and that abuse can contribute to bulimia, bingeing, and anorexia.[4] While sexual abuse does not automatically result in an eating problem, and having an eating problem does not necessarily mean that a woman has been sexually abused, studies do suggest that more women with eating problems have been sexually abused than women who do not have eating problems.

This research offers important insights about the impact of sexual abuse on eating problems. Sexual victimization can cause body-image disturbances, mistrust of one's experiences, confusion about bodily sensations, negative self-esteem, and difficulties in identifying or knowing one's feelings.[5] Dieting, bingeing, and purging are all ways women respond to these disturbances. Dieting can help a woman re-gain control of her body, which is lost during sexual abuse. Women may try to "get rid of" their bodies—which they see as bad as a con-sequence of abuse—by purging.[6] Bulimia anesthetizes painful feelings and helps dissipate anger, but also justifies feelings of unworthiness and self-hatred. Bulimia is also one way women cleanse themselves of sexual assault and establish "psychological and physical boundaries between [themselves] and the rest of the world."[7]

Sexual violation can alter a woman's relationship to her body to such an extent that she no longer believes herself to have a body or has trouble staying "in" her body. The process of leaving the body during sexual abuse through numbing and denial parallels that of leaving the body through a binge.[8] Many women initially leave their bodies un-consciously, but this "leaving" can be replicated through bingeing in order to cope with painful experiences, including memories of abuse.[9] As a consequence of sexual abuse, women often lose the sense of their bodies as intact or "in one piece." Replacing images of bodily integrity are graphic metaphors of a body as a "piece of Swiss cheese," as an "eggshell that has been smashed into a thousand pieces," as "ashes thrown up in the air, no shape at all."[10] The dissociation resulting from sexual abuse leaves women vulnerable to using food, alcohol, or other substances to maintain the "leaving the body" experience. Their use of food to cope with sexual abuse reveals complicated and nu-anced insights into why women often suffer abuse alone, how their cultural and racial identities shape their responses to abuse, and how eating problems may begin as a way women get on with their lives.

Stolen Bodies, Stolen Dreams

Some of the most startling and painful realities in women's lives are the numerous psychic and physical assaults they often face as children. Two-thirds of the women I interviewed are survivors of sexual abuse, a proportion similar to that found in other studies of women with eating problems.[11] The majority had been sexually abused by more than one person, and almost all of the perpetrators were men. The women are from a variety of socioeconomic classes and races, a finding also consistent with most studies on sexual abuse.[12]

Of the women who were sexually abused, most were victims of incest.[13] Their average age when incest began was seven; duration ranged from two occasions to more than ten years. All of the abuse involved physical contact, which ranged from rubbing and kissing to rape. For all of the survivors of incest, victimization was their first exposure to sexual contact. Rape meant, in Rosalee's words, "being in the embarrassing situation of not being a virgin when I should have been a virgin." It is a chilling reality for a staggering number of girls that sexual activity is equated with violence and violation long before they are introduced to life-affirming sexual activity based on mutual consent.

Because most of the survivors I interviewed had only recently remembered being abused, they were just beginning to examine how the experience contributed to their eating problems. (Repression of memories of sexual abuse is common; the average age when women remember being violated is between twenty-nine and forty-nine.)[14] I was struck by the women's rich metaphors and explanations of connections between sexual abuse and eating problems—particularly since so many of their memories of abuse were new. While the type of sexual abuse varied, many of them used food—often the only method available to them at the time—to cope.

RUTHIE: "I saw myself as that flat little kid who played handball."

Ruthie is a thirty-four-year-old Puerto Rican woman who developed eating problems in the form of bulimia, dieting, and compulsive eating when she was fourteen years old. As a child, she was the thinnest of the eight daughters in her family. Ruthie liked her body and, despite her mother's attempts to fatten her, she remained thin through puberty. When she was twelve her godmother's father began to molest her and continued to do so until she was sixteen. He frequently forced her to touch him and molested her in her bed and outside of her house. She tried to run away from him, pleaded with her mother not to make her stay at his house, and sometimes "cussed him out." But he was bigger than she was and used physical force to get his way. The respect given to godparents in Puerto Rican communities and the fact that he lived downstairs from Ruthie's family made it hard for her to avoid him.

Ruthie's sense of her body changed dramatically when he began to molest her. Although she weighed only 100 pounds, she began to feel fat and thought what she interpreted as fat was to blame for his abusing her. Having always liked her thin body, she hated this change. She also resented puberty, interpreting breasts and hips as fat. She said, "getting the shape of a woman was really traumatic for me. So I just didn't want to do that, didn't want to develop. I just wanted to be that free-spirited kid that I was." She had seen a movie on television about Romans who made themselves throw up, and she began to do it, hoping that she could look and feel like the "little kid" again. Her symbolic attempt to protect herself by purging stands in stark contrast to the psychoanalytic explanation of eating problems as an "abnormal" repudiation of sexuality. In fact, her actions and those of many other survivors of sexual abuse represent a logical attempt at self-protection by seeking a size and a shape that do not seem as vulnerable to sexual assault.

In response to sexual abuse, Ruthie detached from her body, as is typical of many people who have faced trauma directed at the body; leaving the body is one way of coping "when the body is not a safe place to be."[15] Ruthie says:

> I didn't want to deal with what was going on in my body. And what this guy was doing. And how my body was developing. So in a lot of ways I detached. In a lot of ways I saw myself still as that flat little kid that used to play handball.

By throwing up after she ate anything she considered fattening, she thought she could make herself into the child she used to be. Purging allowed her to maintain a split between the child who was safe—the one who played handball before the molestation began—while detaching from the adult body that was under siege. Thus purging was a symbolic attempt to hold on to the unviolated child and at the same time it allowed her to eat what she wanted.

When Ruthie was sixteen, the man died and she stopped purging. The day before he died, he tried to molest her while she was playing outside. In her mind, his death had become her only protection since she had found no other way to stop him. She stared directly into his face and told him to "drop dead." The next day he did just that, falling down on the street in front of Ruthie and dying. No one knew exactly what caused his death, but in Ruthie's mind she had willed it and was impressed by her power. Both the end of the abuse and Ruthie's feelings of power contributed to the end of her bulimia.

She remained worried about her weight and body size, however, in part as a response to sexual harassment by friends and relatives. In one instance, when she was stalked by a man, she ran to her house, only to be told by her parents that she was to blame. Describing how she felt, she says, "It was pretty tough around that time. I was saying, I am not even developed. What do they want with me?" By the time she was sixteen she had lost an accurate sense of her shape and size. The fact that her mother had done an about-face, first giving her appetite stimulants and then beating her during adolescence while telling her to diet, contributed to her uncertainty about her body. In voicing a confusion typical of many survivors of sexual abuse, Ruthie says, "I don't even know what I was. I know I wasn't fat. But I felt fat. To me I was fat." Partly in response to this puzzling view of her body, Ruthie began to diet, feeling guilty when she ate rich food and constantly weighing herself.

JOSELYN: *"My body is just like ashes thrown up in the air, just no shape at all."*

Joselyn, a thirty-five-year-old African-American woman, endured several sexual invasions in addition to emotional and physical abuse when she was a child, leaving her with a fragmented notion of who she was and no sense of having a body. When I asked her about her image of her body, Joselyn said:

> I have never had a picture of what I look like. I could dream but I could never dream about myself. I could never see myself. . . . To this day I could shut my eyes and not know what I look like. I was always just like ashes thrown up in the air, just no shape at all.

One of the most significant factors in Joselyn's ghostly sense of herself was the physical abuse she endured when she was four, seven, and ten years old. When Joselyn was four, her grandmother used to make a big tub of dishwater and use it to give Joselyn enemas, a ritual she hated and protested.[16] Her white grandmother thought Joselyn was too fat, too dark-skinned, and not pretty, and she played out this racism and sexism on Joselyn's body. She also interpreted Joselyn's normal bodily functions as dirty and wrong and said enemas were a way to "clean [her] out."[17]

When Joselyn was seven, a female friend of her mother's began to molest her. Partly because everyone told Joselyn that being fat was bad, she thought this woman was molesting her because of her size. Since her parents told her she was to blame for her size, she thought she caused the molestation. She didn't tell anyone what had occurred, and, until two years prior to our interview, "forgot" about it. When she was ten, her (male) math tutor began to molest her. As before, she thought that it was because of her size. Voicing her confusion, she says, "I had mixed feelings. I had people telling me being thin is how you should be to get a man, but it seemed like I got this man putting his hand up my skirt."

This mixed message made it hard for Joselyn to have a realistic sense of her body size and shape. The size Joselyn had come to identify as chunky as a result of her parents' and grandmother's constant appraisal of her as fat was actually her body developing: "You know, I was beginning to get breasts, and so I was equating and still equate being heavier with being more sexual." In her mind, "looking sort of womanly" and "beginning to get breasts" were the reasons her tutor molested her. She remembers that "he was such a sleazebag, I can't figure out how they hired him in the first place. To look at him frightened me on first look." But when she told her mother she was scared of him, her mother took no steps to intervene. A key theme in Joselyn's experience, and one echoed by many others, is that children often sense that certain people are not safe. But without protection from adults, this knowledge does little to keep them from harm.

The devastation of sexual abuse was coupled with physical and emotional abuse from her father. He castigated her for being a girl instead of a boy, told her she was fat and ugly, and, when she was unhappy, said she was responsible for her own misery. She remembers many scenes of humiliation and physical abuse. One time she got excited about playing softball with her father only to find that when he chose people to be on his team, he didn't choose her. He routinely beat her with a belt while her mother retreated into another room. She remembers when she was thirteen looking at him and saying, "You should have been born white." When he asked her why, she explained, "Because you could have been a slaveholder. . . . You are so good with that whip it is a shame to just limit it to me."

Joselyn began to blame herself and her body for the abuse she was enduring. She transferred to her body the feelings, ideas, and memories that derived from or were directed at the people who caused the abuse. Her body, rather than the injustice, became the enemy. And now, she says, "I have the same shame around my body that I had when I was ten."

When she was eleven, Joselyn began to use laxatives to lose weight, and she became increasingly worried about being fat. At thirteen, she went on her first diet even though she was thin (five feet eight inches tall and 123 pounds), initiating a cycle of weight loss and gain, bingeing and starving, that continued for many years. In her upwardly mobile family, being thin was associated with acceptance in white society. When classism, racism, and sexual abuse collided, Joselyn's body became the target of her anger and, in her mind, the reason for her unhappiness. The real causes went unnamed. It is only as an adult that she has uncovered what caused her to feel ashamed of her body.

GILDA: *"I did not lose my memory. It was stolen."*

Gilda is a twenty-one-year-old Jewish woman who has compulsively eaten and dieted since she was sixteen. She began bingeing as a consequence of being raped. When she was eleven, the owner of a nightclub tricked her into coming into a back room at his club and then raped her. Afterwards, with the seeming nonchalance commonly shown by people who are in traumatic shock, Gilda says she "got myself together, brushed my hair and walked home. I said hi to my parents and kissed them both good night and went to bed. That is the last thing I remember." She promptly forgot about the rape until five years later, when she began to have horrible nightmares. After remembering the rape she began to eat and gained 110 pounds within a year.

The reason Gilda initially kept the rape a secret and then "forgot" about it can be at least partially traced to confusing messages she had learned about culture and gender. When she was five her family was forced to leave North Africa after several family members were murdered as a consequence of anti-Semitic persecution. When he came to the United States, her father tried to distance himself from his roots as a black Jewish man:

> My father never saw himself as a Third World man. If anything, now I am an American and I was born in [North Africa] and that is my bad luck. He has really pulled himself away in terms of poverty and stereotypes of Third World people, in terms of what it means to be a black Jew. He won't call on that oppression or acknowledge it as a reality.

Her father's denial of his racial identity and the persecution his family endured shaped his confusing attitudes about raising a daughter. Having been brought up in North Africa, he believed that girls needed protection and should never go out alone. Protecting his daughter's virginity was his first concern, and he thought the United States was unsafe, especially for females. While keeping an excessive watch over her in the United States, he permitted her total freedom when the family traveled in Israel, which he believed was an inherently safe place. His reaction to anti-Semitism was to romanticize Israel and Jewish culture.

When Gilda was raped in Israel, she was confused about how to respond. She had been taught to fear American men and respect Israeli men, especially older Jewish men. Yet an older Israeli man had raped her. Because her father idolized Israel, Gilda was not taught that what is dangerous is not certain cultures, but rather individual men—from any culture—who rape women. When the assault occurred, her sense of right and wrong was blurred. Mixed messages about racism and anti-Semitism fueled her confusion about injustice:

> I had so many mixed messages about right and wrong as I grew up. On the one hand, I had people calling me kike at school. On the other hand, my father would be calling people niggers in the house. He said it was wrong to call Jews kikes and then used the same language about other people. I didn't know if it was right or wrong to say that this happened to me. I was afraid that my father would let me have it. It was crazy.

In retrospect, she believes the confusion left her silent about the rape.

Gilda went through two stages of reaction to the rape. As she understands it now, she unconsciously considered rape an "introduction to womanhood" and a forewarning about adult female sexuality. She began "dressing in tight jeans and showing more than I had." Before the rape, she had little interest in boys, preferring to play games and run around. Afterwards, she flirted with boys and men and, at fourteen, became sexually active, even though her parents forbade it. At thirteen she left home for a couple of weeks. She began to defy her father openly, smoking marijuana, drinking alcohol, and staying out late. Her male-centered, trouble-making actions were partly her attempt to gain control over sexuality and sexual encounters. Like some other survivors of sexual abuse, Gilda dressed in revealing ways and devoted considerable energy to finding and pleasing boyfriends as a way to contradict the powerlessness of being raped.[18]

The second stage of her reaction to the rape occurred after she remembered it. At sixteen she began to have nightmares and cried often. As a child and a teenager she had been thin, and although she had been teased about her lanky shape, she liked her body. When she remembered the rape, she began to gain weight rapidly. During the year she gained 110 pounds, she went from constantly wanting to look "hot for the young guys" to feeling completely indifferent about men. As is typical among survivors in the early stages of healing, she swung between two extremes, from dressing and acting in a highly sexualized way (to assert some control over her sexuality) to hiding her attractiveness (in order to avoid further sexual objectification).[19] Gaining weight made her feel that she was protected from male attention:

> I didn't want to look like the women in the magazines. I didn't want to have breasts that everyone saw. I wanted to have breasts for myself. I wanted to have something that was mine. Something that they couldn't take . . . by being fat, no one would be attracted to me, but I could have breasts for myself that would be hidden by the fat.

Gilda interpreted fat as a protection against others' appropriation of her body. Gaining weight did not indicate fear of her female body, as some theorists would maintain, but rather an attempt to protect herself and to claim her body as her own.

Like many other survivors of sexual abuse, she developed complicated ideas about her body. On the one hand, she was comforted by the weight gain, particularly since it seemed to make her less vulnerable to men's prurient interests. And yet in other ways she was out of touch with her body, specifically in terms of her changing size. When her mother expressed surprise at the sudden weight gain, saying she couldn't believe it was her, Gilda said that she didn't think her body was hers either. She still saw herself as "this bony little thing" — the girl she had been before the rape. Like many women, Gilda had an image of her body before it was violated. The rape had disrupted her sense of her body, leaving her out of touch with the dramatic changes in her size. As Gilda was searching for a realistic sense of her body, she distanced herself from her family's eating traditions. Before she remembered the rape, her family had always eaten together, an activity her father considered key to maintaining his Jewish and North African cultural heritage. Eating had always been a family event; there had been no such thing as grabbing something to eat or snacking between meals, and no one ever ate alone. In defiance, Gilda started to eat constantly, abruptly disturbing family customs. She began to buy food in stores and restaurants and eat alone in her room. Explaining her new patterns of eating, Gilda says:

> My father had frightened me about eating anything out of the home because it is not kosher. You could get diseases and who knows where the food comes from. . . . In [North Africa] there was no notion of ready-to-go food. There was no [stopping] somewhere [to] get a meal. You had to buy stuff, take it home, and prepare it. It was a process. Soak it. Treat it. Clean it. There was no grab-it-and-go. When I was sixteen I found grab-it-and-go. It was a crazy time.

Her father was infuriated, interpreting her actions as yet another way she was not being a good daughter.

Her rebellion stymied her parents. Her calls for help—evident in her sudden weight gain and behavior changes—were unintelligible to her parents, which made it impossible for them to help her. But gaining weight did afford her some psychological protection from sexual objectification, and eating what and when she wanted to made her feel as if she had some power:

> I could eat when I wanted to. Eating alone was so great. I could eat by myself. I could eat whatever I wanted, whenever I wanted without anyone telling me what I could do. It was [a] time when I had total control over myself.

After remembering the rape, she had a hard time trusting people, especially her father. Once she understood that some of her father's strictures were contradictory—that he prohibited her from going out with friends in the United States yet set no limits in Israel—she was no longer willing to accept any of the lessons he had taught her or trust his authority. After regaining her memory, she no longer trusted any men. Meanwhile, the man with whom she was in a relationship had begun to abuse her, breaking her ribs, kidnapping her, and to mistreat her emotionally. Her estrangement from her family, coupled with her boyfriend's abuse, made it hard for her to trust anyone. Food became her trusted companion. She says:

> How do you know what to take seriously? If you are not feeling like you trust people and you are not really trusting yourself, there has to be some way to regain some sense of trust. Control and trust seem to be similar things. . . . Food won't fail you. Food won't give you mixed messages. You eat too much. It makes you feel a certain way. You don't eat enough, it makes you feel a certain way. Food is pretty consistent in terms of being able to rely upon it. When you talk about availability, it makes me think about how lucky I was to have that and not crack. You know?

DAWN: *"I . . . used drugs, food, and alcohol for years to deny my feelings."*

Dawn is a twenty-nine-year-old white middle-class woman who, when I talked with her, had been recovering for fifteen months from bulimia and anorexia—plus addiction to alcohol, cocaine, Valium, and speed. She grew up in an upper middle class Boston suburb and was raised by both of her parents, who are of Italian descent. Her problems with food began when she was very young. She remembers visiting a friend's house when she was eight and eating a second dinner even though she wasn't hungry. Her mother restricted the amount of food that her daughters could eat while allowing her sons to eat all they wanted, and she taught her daughters that being fat was the single worst attribute a girl could have. When Dawn was eight or nine years old her mother suggested that Dawn accompany her eleven-year-old sister to Weight Watchers. Dawn went because, as she says, "I have this confusion in my own head that even though I was skinny [and] I could look at myself and think that I was thin, I actually had to really be careful and diet." At twelve, even though she weighed only 105 pounds (and was five feet three inches tall), her mother admonished her that she should watch her weight more carefully. That year Dawn made herself throw up for the first time because she had binged and felt bad about it. Her mother was constantly on a diet even though she was not fat. Her sister threw up regularly after meals into a large coffee cup she carried with her. The entire family—Dawn's four siblings and their parents—would sit together in the den after dinner and say nothing as her sister threw up into her cup. The silence was palpable.

In addition to linking her eating problems to her family's emphasis on dieting, Dawn has also begun to attribute them to sexual abuse by her father, an uncle, and two men in the neighborhood. Although Dawn only recently began to recover memories of sexual abuse, she increasingly believes that her addiction to food and drugs helped her "deny whatever feelings I had" and, at their core, signified self-hatred caused by the sexual abuse. Her uncle began to abuse her when she was eight years old, the same year she began to binge and to worry about her weight. She knew at the time that she was being violated and that her "whole body was tense." Yet when she told her older brothers and sisters, they said she was lying. Then her uncle violated her sister, too, so at least one other person acknowledged that it had indeed happened. By the time she was thirteen, Dawn was bingeing regularly, eating frozen food out of the freezer and stealing money for food and drugs. During adolescence she began to use speed and cocaine.

While bingeing helped her deny her feelings, dieting gave her a sense of control. Since she had been raised to believe that healthy appetites were dangerous and that she would be rewarded for weight loss, dieting helped her feel powerful. She remembers "lingering over a chocolate shake to make it last longer." Purging was both a way to insure that she would stay thin and a response to her confusion about her body size. At the time the sexual abuse began, Dawn lost a realistic sense of her body shape and size. By the time she was twelve, she was struggling to know what her body looked like, asking herself "Am I

fat? Am I thin? Am I fat? Am I thin? One day I would think I was fat
and needed to be on a diet. The next day I looked thin." Because she
had no reliable sense of her actual body size, she panicked when she
gained a few pounds. During high school she weighed between 115
and 130 pounds:

> When I weighed 115 to 120 I was outgoing, confident. I could pick
> any guy, I could be with anybody. I still remember, though, being that
> thin, having a lot of fears. But I looked good so I felt better about
> myself. When I was up toward 130, I was a basket case. I would
> sneak into school . . . I had tremendous self-hatred.

As a consequence of sexual abuse, she had little faith in her power
over her own bodily integrity: protection from unwanted touch, control of food intake, and regulation of bodily functions. Once she began
to have sexual intercourse, when she was fourteen, she often became
suddenly repulsed and had "shameful get-away feelings" after having
an orgasm. Then she would feel desperate to be alone and push her
partner away. As an adult, she still feels ashamed sometimes when she
is being sexual and has only recently begun to understand the connections between her shame and childhood sexual abuse. By later adolescence, she used bingeing as a way to put the brakes on in a sexual relationship. After being sexually involved with a man for a period of
time, she would suddenly wake up one morning and be repulsed that
she was with him. She would begin to binge and, in her words, "the
more I binged, the more hateful I became, the more of a bitch I became
. . . bingeing would let me break off a relationship." By bingeing she
stopped being sexually available and responded to the threat to her
bodily integrity that was originally caused by sexual abuse and was
triggered by sexual activity. Paradoxically, however, bingeing also disrupted her bodily integrity, since feeling full and bloated made her feel
panicked and invaded once more.

Dawn also had difficulty feeling attached to her body or to the
world. When I asked her if she resided inside of her body during adolescence and adulthood, she responded, "I had no conception of myself as a person, as a human being related to the world." By sixteen she
was running away from home for days at a time and "shooting dope
with the junkie down the street":

> I would bring him a dime bag of crystal mescaline and he had a
> syringe and would get me off. He would shoot me up with dope. I
> would save a little bit for him and I would do him and would leave.

When she was sixteen her mother found syringes in her bathroom but
decided they did not belong to Dawn. That same year, her father

caught her boyfriend sneaking out of Dawn's window one morning after they had been shooting dope all night long. Dawn's father didn't say anything about the incident.

The signs that Dawn was in trouble continued to go unnoticed as her drug addiction and bulimia worsened. Despite the obvious, her family never intervened—a clear case of denial. Like many of the other women I interviewed, Dawn developed eating problems when her other pleas for help were not heard. Her alcoholic father was not emotionally available to his children:

> I did not know my father. I saw him. My memory is of him sitting
> on the couch. A gorgeous man with a gorgeous smile and a beautiful
> presence but there was nothing there. There was such a wall. There
> was such denial in my family.

Her mother was overburdened with five children and a rocky marriage. Dawn remembers getting laryngitis when she was three years old, an affliction that she had for much of her childhood. At the time, her mother was pregnant with her fourth child, had three babies under three years old, and was caring for her ill sister's three small children. When Dawn couldn't speak, her mother took her to a doctor who said the laryngitis came from screaming for attention. As Dawn says:

> I was creating all these situations acting out in various ways. I was
> also reaching out for help from very young. At age three I got a
> doctor to see there was a problem in my family. I still have problems
> with my voice.

The fact that Dawn used illegal drugs for years without being stopped by family members, neighbors, or police may be related to her gender and race. Had she lived in an African-American or Latino neighborhood and been male, her drug use probably would have caused her legal problems. As it was, she was never arrested, but no one ever helped her, either.

ROSALEE: *"Raisins and smiles for me and my sister."*

Rosalee is a thirty-six-year-old African-American woman who links her compulsive eating to childhood traumas including incest and other sexual abuse. When she was young, Rosalee lived on various army bases in Europe but spent most of her growing-up years in a rural community in Arkansas. She grew up in a violent household: her alcoholic father beat her mother constantly, and Rosalee was beaten by both of her parents. As Rosalee explains it, she was born a survivor:

I was born in extreme poverty. My mother married my father and
that lasted about six months until he found out she was pregnant.
That's the story I was told. And then he took her home to her mom
way out in the woods in Arkansas and he took off for two years.
That was kind of how we got started, through her depression. My
grandmother once told me that my mother had tried to jump off a
porch when she was pregnant with me under the stress of it all. If my
grandmother remembered correctly, I am a real toughy 'cause I hung
in there. Those were the early things I got from the beginning.

Rosalee's first memories are of her fourth year, when a white man
who frequently took care of her, a "family friend," began to molest
her. Although she can't remember all of the details, she knows the
abuse went on for several years and involved rape. By the time she was
five, her father had also started to rape her, which he continued to do
regularly until she reached puberty. She thinks he stopped abuse that
involved contact when she reached puberty, but he continued to expose himself to her throughout her high school years. When she was
twelve she was also sexually abused on one occasion by another "family friend."

Like many abused children, Rosalee tried a number of tactics to
stop the abuse. When her baby-sitter began to molest her, she told her
mother that "my little thing bothered me," but her mother told her she
shouldn't be touching it—effectively laying the blame for vaginal pain
on Rosalee. Rosalee told her mother she didn't like the man, but her
mother said, "I heard you laughing. I heard you playing" with him.
What sounded like playing to her mother was the man tickling and
then molesting her. When her father began to rape her, she tried, to no
avail, to run away or scream for her mother.

During the years that her father and the "family friend" were abusing her, she had many physical symptoms that she now associates with
those experiences: bed wetting, migraine headaches, memory lapses,
severe depression, suicidal feelings, and nightmares.[20] When she was
very young, she remembers hysterically going into her mother's bedroom and asking her to come see the bogey man that was trying to get
Rosalee. When she began to develop migraines and cry for days at a
time, her mother was unable to cope with it: "She felt she could beat
me and it would be all right," and she said that beating Rosalee would
give her a "real reason to cry."

Rosalee's siblings weren't able to help, either. In fact, Rosalee
learned only recently that her father was molesting her younger sister
too. As is common in families where incest is occurring, it is difficult
for siblings to help each other because of denial or fear of reprisal.
Partly because Rosalee's family moved around so much, she never

made a connection with anyone outside the family with whom she could comfortably talk. Her classmates in Arkansas nicknamed her "Oreo cookie"—black on the outside and white inside. Since she had lived in Germany and other European countries when she was young, she talked and acted differently than the black children who had lived in the South all their lives. While her "differences" made it hard for her to fit in with black classmates, fitting in with white children was no easier.

Rosalee was never able to get help—the obstacles of her father's authoritative control in the family, his beating her mother, and the isolation that came from moving around so often were too great—so she did whatever she could do to comfort herself, and much of it was eating. Rosalee saw eating as a way to soothe herself as far back as she can remember:

> I think I was bingeing when I was really young, although I wouldn't have used those terms. I would have said eating like a pig. It would sedate me, I would feel like life is good. Yeah. Food gives me a high ... I would have in no way thought about it in terms of a sedation or a high. I know I felt good when there was plenty of food around. If I couldn't sleep I could always eat and it was something I could do by myself.

When Rosalee was a young child, she didn't know the reasons she ate more than other people, got up in the middle of the night to eat, or hid food that she might want later. Looking back, Rosalee now says:

> Food sedated me. It helped me sleep. To help me feel somehow fortified so that if my mother woke up and maybe she was too pissed to fix breakfast, I had something in my stomach. Or if she and dad were going to get fighting or something like that I had something to hold me. That was part of my eating. It was a way to comfort ourselves.

In Rosalee's poor family, having food in the house was a sign of celebration; people would eat a lot to make up for leaner times. Thus food was Rosalee's friend, not something that she was told was bad or needed to be controlled.

As Rosalee endured various forms of victimization, she began to sneak food, saving it for hard times. "Kids," she says, "do their best to find a way to play through tension"—and eating was her way of playing:

> If my sister got a beating or she was afraid because of the fighting or couldn't go to sleep, it was all I knew to do that would take our minds off of it. I'd make little faces. We used to get the preserves that had little grapes in it. [She laughs.] You have your jelly and then you

have your preserves. The preserves had fruit in it. So I'd make happy faces. Raisins and smiles for me and my sister.

Bingeing was a creative coping mechanism in the face of terrible odds. When there was food in the house, Rosalee could get it without having to rely on any adults. She would eat so much that she could barely sit up. Eventually, her stomach would hurt so badly that she would lie down on the floor and stop eating. As a drug, food worked quickly to help her "stuff back emotions."

It has been a relief for Rosalee to begin to uncover the memories of sexual abuse, but making sense of them is a painful task. Even at thirty-six, she is not yet able to identify herself as a survivor of incest:

> I haven't been in that place of feeling like I have actually survived it. I feel like it is kicking my ass right now. To bring up that kind of pain. I would literally fall apart. . . . I still feel a lot of shame about it. I feel an awful amount of hurt. How could someone do that? I found this little suit that I wore. It was hand made in Germany. One of my favorite suits and my molester always liked seeing me in it. I found it one day when I was cleaning up my closet. When I saw how small it was, I freaked out. I just freaked out. I didn't have a chance in hell. I just didn't have a chance.

ANTONIA: *If you don't have any coping mechanisms, you eat.*"

Antonia is a thirty-five-year-old Italian-American woman who has had problems with compulsive eating since she was four years old. She has often wondered why she ate compulsively in early childhood, and she recently recovered "emotional memories" of being sexually abused by her grandfather when she was four. By "emotional memories" she means that she has remembered the emotions connected with being sexually abused; she cannot yet remember the details.

As a toddler, Antonia was big and tall, but not fat. When she was four, her parents sent her to stay with her grandparents in Florida for the summer. When Antonia's mother came to get her a month later, she took one look at Antonia and "burst into tears because I looked like a little brown butterball. That is what she called me." Although Antonia blocked the memories at the time, she now realizes that her grandfather had been sexually molesting her and that one way she responded was to eat. Beginning that summer and for many years after, Antonia often woke up during the middle of the night with anxiety attacks and nightmares.

Bingeing, she says, made her "disappear," which made her feel protected; it began as a way to numb and block painful feelings. She describes bingeing as a nurturing act, a way of feeding herself when she was scared: "What else do you do? If you don't have any coping mechanisms, you eat." Like many women who began to binge when they were young, Antonia was not always fully conscious as she did it. When she ate during the night it was

> like sleep walking. . . . It was mostly desperate like I had to have it . . . I keep coming to that sense that it would make me go away. I didn't care after that. I didn't care. [So you could go back to sleep? I asked.] Yeah. It is not really even physically waking up. . . . It doesn't seem to have anything to do with how much I eat or what I eat . . . I would just have to go to bed. I would just literally have to go to bed and pass out. But it is mostly about going away. The second I reach for something I am gone. That would make a lot of sense if you feel like you have to disappear.

Bingeing was Antonia's response to the split caused by trauma. When the sexual abuse occurred, Antonia felt she had lost her body. In her mind, the body she lived in afterwards was not really hers. Antonia described herself as "not . . . the girl I was before the abuse. The girl who was abused was someone else." In this description, Antonia identifies the process of splitting or dissociation by which a person separates consciousness from body, or "leaves the body."[21] It begins as a way to protect oneself from trauma, a way of removing oneself from the location of pain. Initially, it is possible to dissociate at will, but to maintain dissociation over time, it is necessary to use a substance such as food or alcohol.[22] Dissociation may begin as a coping technique but develop into an autonomous symptom. A person may dissociate mind from body to escape the pain of sexual victimization and eventually use this method of "leaving the body" to escape other traumas and stressful situations.[23]

Antonia began to binge at night after she had a nightmare and couldn't go back to sleep. Some of the nightmares may have been memories she had repressed because she did not yet have the support she needed to deal with them. Bingeing sedated her and made her feel as if she "didn't exist." In a way, she didn't: the integrated Antonia had been destroyed. Just as her mother could not believe that the chubby girl who greeted her at the end of the summer was Antonia, Antonia no longer saw herself as she had once been:

> This wasn't me that he was doing this to and I will show you why it wasn't me. Because I don't look like me anymore . . . I felt like I wasn't me for the rest of my life.

The girl her grandfather was abusing was not her (the thin girl). The girl being molested was someone else (the fat girl). To protect herself, Antonia split into two parts—her consciousness (the thin girl) and her fat body (the one being molested). Bingeing ensured Antonia the split that was necessary to keep the memories repressed. By sedating her, it allowed her to repress memories too painful to acknowledge. The fat was the physical proof that the girl Antonia's mother once knew had been destroyed. Bingeing then reconfirmed that the thin girl was not there. As Antonia says, "If you don't believe you exist then it is very comforting to be doing something that makes you not exist."

The fact that Antonia binged rather than dieted in response to trauma also made sense since she saw little reason to try to be petite, as girls were supposed to be. Growing up as one of only a few Italian-Americans in a Protestant town where most people were of Northern European descent, Antonia felt that everything from her weight to the dark hair on her upper lip were out of place. From an early age, she knew she "never embodied the essence of the good girl. I don't like her, I have never acted like her. I can't be like her. I sort of gave up." Antonia's body signified her outsider status.

She knew that other people would consider her eating at night wrong; if she got caught, she would be blamed. She was told that she should be ashamed of being fat, so she told herself that she wasn't going to sneak food, but in the middle of the night she would eat anyway. As she ate, she felt "defiant" and "gross" but unable to stop herself. It was the only way she knew to calm herself and go back to sleep.

Delusional Theories and Missing Pieces

The intricate links women make between being sexually abused and their eating patterns raise the question of why, until recently, so little was known about how eating problems may result from sexual abuse. The answer is partly the dominance of psychoanalysis in models of mental health and illness, and in particular its persistent refusal to consider the centrality of sexual abuse in women's mental health concerns. During the past ten years, a number of researchers have documented the damage caused by Freud's abandonment, in 1897, of his seduction theory, which traced mental illness to repressed memories of sexual abuse, and his subsequent identification of his patients' memories of sexual abuse as delusional fantasies.[24]

Freud's reversal and its widespread impact on psychological theory has significantly hindered attention to the role of sexual abuse in depression, schizophrenia, agoraphobia, and other mental health concerns, including eating problems.[25] The dominance of the psychoanalytic model in studies of eating problems in the 1940s and 1950s effectively obfuscated links to sexual abuse by attributing anorexia and bulimia to unconscious concerns about "oral impregnation." Anorexics, so the theory went, are unable to come to terms with adult sexuality (assumed to be heterosexuality), an inability played out in part through an unconscious interpretation of eating as a form of oral impregnation to be avoided at any cost.[26] Bulimics, the theory continued, have oral impregnation fantasies that they try to satisfy by bingeing.

Feminists have now documented cases in which psychiatrists ignored the influence of incest among anorexic patients. Even women who told their psychiatrists they had been abused were told that their anorexia was "a defense against incestuous wishes for father," "a defense against oral impregnation fantasies and an unconscious pregnancy wish," "an angry gesture toward a parental figure."[27] These explanations deeply confuse and blur power relations, effectively blaming women for their eating problems while translating a woman's fear of rape into a fear of the desire to be raped. At the same time, the psychiatrists' explanations ignore the perpetrators' incestuous behavior, despite data from the doctors' own records that reveal incest.

The psychoanalytic focus on problematic mother-daughter relations has also blurred connections between sexual abuse and eating problems. Psychoanalytic literature is shot through with the notion that anorexic girls have domineering, overprotective, and controlling mothers. According to this logic, a girl develops anorexia partly as a defensive reaction to domination, revealing an unconscious ambivalence toward or hatred of her mother.[28] Whether or not this conflict does exist, there is almost no mention of fathers' roles in families in general and their participation in raising daughters specifically. There is neither attention to a father's potentially positive influence on his daughter's relationship to food and her body nor recognition of how a father may be implicated in a daughter's discomfort with her body, despite the fact that the vast majority of cases of incest involve female children and male adults.[29] Alice Miller writes that "the psychoanalytic goal is to uphold the defense mechanisms of generations of fathers."[30] Thus the limitation in the psychoanalytic literature on eating problems is part of a larger theoretical exclusion and cover-up of male violence. Therapists Maria Root and Patricia Fallon explain that

> perhaps the denial and rationalization our socio-political systems
> have demonstrated in response to abuse against women in our culture
> is reflected in the reluctance of researchers in the field of eating
> disorders to collect conflictual and potentially controversial data.[31]

Feminist researchers have had to confront this history of obfuscation as they have documented how sexual abuse may make women vulnerable to eating problems. Why feminist research on incest and eating problems has only recently emerged also reflects a general pattern in feminist research on violence against women. While feminist studies of sexual assault in the 1970s primarily examined violence in the public sphere and against adult women—sexual harassment and sexual assault, for example—it wasn't until the 1980s that research on incest emerged. It took longer to uncover sexual abuse of girls committed within the privacy, isolation, and secrecy of the family. The recent studies of connections between incest and eating problems parallels stages in feminist research on sexual abuse in general. In addition, the stereotype of eating problems as concern about appearance also slowed recognition of women as survivors of trauma rather than victims of male models of beauty.

Echoing Silences

The courage of survivors and the dedication of feminist scholars in the past decade has at last made it impossible to ignore the epidemic of abuse. The combination of activism and scholarship has also encouraged examination of the psychological and sociological dynamics of eating problems among survivors of sexual abuse. Feminists have rejected the notion that memories of sexual abuse are merely the products of delusional fantasies and identified reasons why women cope with sexual trauma by bingeing or dieting. The women I interviewed confirmed how bulimia, anorexia, and bingeing begin as logical responses to sexual abuse and explained multiple reasons why—both historically and currently—they have been forced to deal with this abuse alone. It is the isolation and loneliness that remain characteristic of sexual abuse that make anorexia and bulimia seemingly logical responses.

Most of the women I talked with grew up before the current feminist wave of popular and scholarly books on sexual abuse, and their relatives did not recognize their bed wetting, nightmares, eating changes, and depression as possible signs of sexual abuse. An eating problem, like these other symptoms, is often a cry for help that may be denied or misunderstood. In this vacuum, bingeing and dieting are solutions because a girl can do them on her own. Whether they stole food from a neighbor's house, hid food, made a chocolate shake last for an hour and a half, or threw up food they didn't want in their bodies, the women I interviewed did these things alone. While those who dieted openly admitted they were rationing their food, the women who binged and purged told no one. Regardless of their coping strategies, they either could not or would not reveal to others how sexual trauma influenced their actions.

Despite increased consciousness in recent years, abuse has not stopped. Public education encouraging children to speak up has done little to ensure that they will be protected. Nationally known cases of mothers who have tried to protect their children from abuse but got no support from the courts underline the fact that public visibility does not necessarily result in social justice.[32] As Louise Armstrong writes, "Those in power are asked to condemn acts so often committed by the members of the power group."[33] Calling out for help may simply bring on another violation. As Gayle Woodsum, an advocate for survivors of sexual abuse, said: "What's happening to the kids is what their offenders told them would happen if they told. If you tell you'll get thrown in jail. Or foster care. Or the mental health system. Or get a publicly endorsed life with an incest offender."[34] Supporters of what they call false memory syndrome have recently formed a national group claiming that parents are being falsely accused of incest. In its ability to garner significant media attention and support from leading psychologists and other health professionals, this organization has fueled a backlash against the activism and research that seek to eradicate sexual abuse.[35] Public awareness has not sufficiently changed the social landscape, and a frightening number of girls still cope with abuse virtually on their own.

The effect of abuse on family dynamics is another reason girls often cope with abuse by themselves. Children typically know that sexual abuse is wrong but do not necessarily have the vocabulary to explain it. Two therapists who work with survivors have said that the predicament is "like being a prisoner in a foreign country and not knowing the language."[36] Many girls remain quiet about incest for fear that talking might jeopardize a sibling's safety. The secret the abused child keeps becomes a barrier to intimacy with her siblings; especially in relationships in which siblings are used to telling each other everything, a secret can create an impossible, inexplicable divide. Secrecy may also be a girl's attempt to protect her mother from pain. Many girls know that their mothers would be devastated to learn that their husbands or lovers are capable of sexual abuse and may be more terrified of hurting their mothers than of anything that could happen to them. Girls who come to believe they are the cause of the abuse are silenced further. This tragic reasoning is nevertheless logical: why tell people about something shameful, especially if you are the one who has caused it?

The enormous discrepancy between the love, tenderness, and respect that a parent is supposed to show and the abuser's selfish conquest of a child's body leaves children blaming themselves. Being abused by someone others respect can seem so incongruous that silence and the repression of memories make complete sense. The women I interviewed often described being abused by men who were admired in their communities and thought of as "family men" — "Uncle Harvey who is gorgeous and wonderful and loved by everyone," the math tutor whom children were taught to respect, trusted family friends. It is easier for a girl to believe that she has the power to cause someone to abuse her than to believe that someone she needs to trust and love is capable of cruel violation. Self-blame and its attendant emotion, shame, are forms of psychic protection.[37] Anger aimed inward is more tolerable than the rage of being abandoned and injured, particularly by a loved one. With this transference, anger and rage are not dealt with directly, but instead become unexplained and diffuse emotions, triggered not only by abuse but by other painful experiences as well. Bingeing, purging, and dieting become a reasonable response to this diffused rage, turned inward in the form of shame. The body becomes a receptacle for this shame, an easy target for distrust and dissatisfaction. Bingeing and maintaining a strict diet are distractions from this pain. The druglike effect of a binge and the high resulting from lack of food also temporarily numb shame and sadness.

The silence enforced by patriarchy and the authority granted to adults may be further reinforced by racism and other oppression. For example, the Sephardic Jewish woman's silence about being raped was reinforced by her father's inconsistent parenting related to religious persecution and anti-Arab discrimination. Ruthie was afraid to reveal abuse by her godmother's father partly because of the power and authority vested in godparents within Puerto Rican culture. The Italian-American woman's silence was reinforced by her grandfather's prestige in the community and leadership in a statewide Italian organization; since she already felt intensely out of place as an Italian-American girl in an overwhelmingly WASP town, speaking out against a pillar of the Italian community was out of the question. Joselyn was unable to stop the enemas partly because of her grandmother's authority within the family and the racism she aimed at Joselyn and her father. Rosalee was isolated at school partially because of racial politics; at home sexual abuse reinforced male domination and internalized racism. Her father abused her sexually while relaying degrading messages about black women. During the same period of time, Rosalee was being abused by a white man whose actions echoed white men's historic sexual abuse of black women. Her early wish that she were white reflected her desire for a status that might rescue her from powerlessness. Rosalee saw being black rather than racism as her problem.

This reality again underlines why finding a way to cope by herself was a logical response: eating was a symbol of agency, of her determination to find a way to survive injustice.

Taking into consideration women's multidimensional identities widens the range of psychological symptoms that may be attributed to sexual abuse.[38] Shame, nightmares, memory gaps, depression, and a disruption of body consciousness may be reactions to sexual abuse common to women across race and class.[39] However, since sexual abuse influences cultural/racial identities, responses to it are shaped by race and culture as well.[40] For example, once Gilda remembered that she had been raped, she began to eat voraciously, a response that directly opposed her family's eating traditions. Her bingeing alone in her room and eating food that was not customarily in her house infuriated her father and distanced her from the family's Jewish and North African rituals. She not only gained weight, she also altered her cultural traditions. Similarly, Rosalee was caught between her father's internalized racism and her community's ideas about beauty. By dieting, she transgressed Southern, rural, and African-American cultural traditions she was raised to accept, which added to her sense of rootlessness.

Whether a child is a toddler or a teenager, victimized for six months or six years, sexual violation shakes up what "home" means—what it feels like to be comfortable and safe with those who are charged with keeping children out of harm's way. Since racial and cultural identity is primarily taught in the home, this socialization process is inevitably disrupted when the home is no longer a refuge, but rather a place of stress and fear. At the same time, sexual abuse makes it precarious for girls to feel at home in their own bodies. Painful emotions and feelings of despair make it risky to be inside of one's body—the very center of threatening feelings. When a girl is robbed of a place that feels safe and relaxed, the world can seem too big, too scary, too hard. It is this daunting situation that author Dorothy Allison describes in *Bastard out of Carolina* when Bone, a child robbed of her innocence by sexual and physical abuse, says, "I tried not to think about how much of an exile I was beginning to feel."[41] Being forced into exile from their own bodies—their homes—leaves children feeling isolated and alone, believing that the injury that has befallen them is uniquely their own and that they are singularly and solely responsible for it. That sexual abuse is epidemic—and therefore neither individually caused nor prevented without collective action—is masked by secrecy and isolation. It is in this context that bingeing, dieting, and purging begin as protective responses to abuse.

4   Hungry and Hurting

It was hunger I felt then, raw and terrible, a shaking deep
down inside me, as if my rage had used up everything I
had ever eaten.

Dorothy Allison[1]

What girls grow up thinking is acceptable—how they can move,
who they can play with, who they can touch, what they can eat
and wear, and who they can trust—is determined as much by their fe-
maleness as by their race, class, and sexuality. Understanding this offers essential clues about why many girls grow up distrusting their
bodies and their appetites and why, when their bodies are belittled and
manipulated, food often becomes their drug of choice. The women I
interviewed not only draw significant connections between sexual
abuse and eating problems, they also link these problems to several
other traumas, including emotional and physical abuse, racism, poverty, heterosexism, and stress caused by acculturation.[2] In this chapter
I chronicle why eating problems begin as reasonable reactions to these
traumas. Their methods of coping underscore why hunger can be experienced both physically and metaphorically, and how rage leaves
women hungry for both food and justice.

Emotional and Physical Abuse

It is virtually impossible to go through a day without hearing about or seeing signs of emotional and physical abuse of children—they are in-justices that cross racial, class, religious, and ethnic lines with aban-don. During the past quarter century, there has been heightened awareness of the prevalence and devastating consequences of child abuse. What is less well known is how children cope with it. A com-bination of commendable attempts to protect children's rights to pri-vacy and confidentiality and the less commendable tendency to listen to adults far longer and more carefully than to children keep us from knowing how children cope with abuse. I have found myself studying the faces of children who have been physically or emotionally injured. I search the newspaper photograph and the television screen for a look, a gaze, or an expression that signals that the child will survive—will find the words, the love, and the tender support a child needs to grow up healthy and strong.

The life-history interviews I conducted reveal myriad ways that girls try to protect themselves from abuse. Many eating problems be-gin as a search for refuge from physical abuse (kicking, slapping, punching, strangling, beating with an object) or emotional abuse (ver-bal insults and accusations, denial of reassurances of being loved and wanted, neglect of basic needs for food and physical touch).[3] All of the women I interviewed who were physically or emotionally abused en-dured abuse for a period of years; often it lasted through an entire childhood and adolescence. Abuse was inflicted by adult caretakers—one or both parents, sometimes in combination with other relatives—and had significant long-term psychological consequences. The wom-en's stories show the logic, creativity, and ingenuity in their use of food to fight the pain of abuse.

ELSA: *"I always felt like my soul was skinny. My soul was free. My soul sort of flew. I was tied down by this big bag of rocks that was my body."*

Elsa is a forty-six-year-old Latina mother who was raised in Argentina and came to the United States with her husband and three children seven years before our interview. She has worried about her weight since she was six years old and has struggled with dieting, bingeing, anorexia, and major weight fluctuations since she was eleven. She was born into an upper-class family and, as is customary among wealthy families in Argentina, was raised by governesses. She had almost no contact with her alcoholic mother until she was ten years old. In Ar-gentina, it was not considered proper for rich women to take care of their children themselves. Elsa says, "Rich people have more power than poor people. They suffer less unless they are extremely rich like when I was a kid. I was deprived emotionally because my family was so rich." She felt rejected by her mother and was deeply dismayed about being cared for by governesses. She thought they hated the job and were only doing the work for economic reasons: "They would talk about their childhoods and how they became poor and how they had to work. I felt really very bad about it. Being a servant in Argentina was kind of the worst thing." She knew that in order to take care of her, they had to leave their own children behind and that they resented her because of this. They told her stories about children they had loved and been separated from, sometimes because of misunderstandings with their employers. The situation was painful for almost everyone involved. Elsa needed love but felt guilty about wanting it.

Elsa also hated the power the governesses had over her body. They would slap her when she wouldn't eat all of her food. She has memories of her nose bleeding and of trying to choke down food while blood was dripping out of her nose. The governesses did not allow her any autonomy. Living at home was like living in military barracks, she says; every aspect of her life was monitored. Each evening, she was subjected to a rigid schedule for completing her homework, bathing, and brushing her teeth—timed almost to the minute. Besides being forced to eat, she was forced to produce a bowel movement every day, even though her metabolism was slow and she was not a very active child. She remembers being five or six years old and being made to sit on the toilet until she was finished, by the caretaker's definition. She says now, "This felt like such a violation. I hated it. I thought it was invasive and disrespectful and so abusive."

Elsa also identified her father's behavior as emotionally abusive. He was a wealthy man who saw his children as

> living off his generosity, his work, his sweat, . . . [as] a bunch of
> babies. A bunch of useless, worthless beings. He gave us all of our
> worth. There wasn't anything intrinsic to us that made us worthy.

From her father's perspective, Elsa was unworthy not only because she was financially dependent but also because she was a girl. Although she was intellectually gifted, because she was a girl her education did not matter to him. From his perspective, all that was important was how she looked. In this she failed miserably because she was fat. Her father yelled at her constantly, which terrified her. Her mother blamed Elsa for his rages, leaving her feeling totally alone. As Elsa puts it, "He was the master of ceremonies and all the rest of us had to obey or pay very dearly for it."

For as long as Elsa can remember, she hated the sexist limitations imposed upon her. Boys could eat more, didn't have a curfew, were supported intellectually, were taken seriously. Being a girl, she thought, meant being like her mother, whom Elsa saw as "a modern-day slave. A geisha." When her mother discovered that Elsa has begun to menstruate, she said, "You poor thing. You've become a woman." Elsa thought:

> If this is being a woman I don't like it. This felt like even more deprivation of freedom than before. This is even worse. A locked-up woman. I felt so much for the Egyptian women in the harems being locked out of life. I hated it.

Elsa was routinely teased because of her weight. Although the asthma that plagued her as a young child eventually subsided, she still had little energy, was chronically exhausted, and gained weight easily. When she became chubby, her parents chastised her and told her she was ugly. She was often teased at school, in stores, and on the street because of her weight. In public she was subjected to insulting questions from strangers who asked if she was pregnant, if there was a reason she was fat, or if there was something wrong with her. Her father told her that "fat was very degenerative and self-indulgent. He had almost a Nazi thing about health and beauty." Her mother was ashamed of having a fat daughter and tried to avoid walking into stores with Elsa, embarrassed to be seen in public with a fat daughter.

At eleven, Elsa was sexually abused by her sister's husband. As is common among victims of sexual abuse, she believed she was abused because she was fat. When she was younger, she had overheard adults talking about men who harassed women in public and how these men preferred chubby girls: "I had this notion that these old perverts like these plump little girls. You heard adults say this too. Sex and flesh being associated." At first, Elsa liked his interest in her; her abuser was the first person who had ever paid much attention to her. But she also felt like a sinner, "the temptress of Babylon," and believed she was responsible for causing this man to be unfaithful to her sister. When she told her mother, the abuse stopped, but her mother told her that if she told anyone else the scandal would ruin her sister's life. Elsa was left feeling guilty, ashamed, and sickened.

Sexual abuse contributed to Elsa's eating problem by adding to her insecurity about her body, since she thought the size of her body caused the abuse. But the despair she felt about her body originated as a consequence of emotional abuse, only to be exacerbated by sexual abuse. Elsa felt guilty about eating before the abuse. More important, she had never had a chance to appreciate her body or understand it as her own.

As a consequence of her beleaguered childhood, Elsa dissociated her soul—which she believed was free and skinny—from her fat and uncontrollable body:

> Remember in school when they talk about the difference between body and soul? I always felt like my soul was skinny. My soul was free. My soul sort of flew. I was tied down by this big bag of rocks that was my body. I had to drag it around. It did pretty much what it wanted and I had a lot of trouble controlling it. It kept me from doing all the things that I dreamed of.

Because Elsa did not know how to vent her anger at the people who hurt her, she made fat the enemy. In her mind, fat was what had "bashed in my dreams." Dieting became her solution, yet being deprived of food eventually led her to binge: "I remember having these bingeing episodes, I felt like I was going to die. Horrendous indigestion. . . . And yet I would do it over and over again." Eating also began as an "emotional filler" as she attempted to make up for the love and support she was not getting. She dieted, lost weight, binged, and dieted until she was fifteen, when her mother took her to a doctor who prescribed amphetamines. This was the first of many times Elsa took prescription drugs to try to shed the fat that she believed was causing her pain.

When Elsa told me that the most important goal in her life is to be thin, I asked her how a woman who had the strength and courage to leave her native country despite her family's protests, divorce her husband, and raise her children as a single mother could, at forty-six, still believe that being thin was the most important goal in her life. She answered my question with a story:

> In a way I was never meant to be fat. I was sort of broken. My world was broken. I was reading about this elephant in San Diego that the trainer had trouble dealing with. She was a female elephant who would not obey the orders. What the trainer did, he and his co-workers, is they beat the elephant over the head with sticks. Not terribly hard, yet enough to cause the skin of the elephant to rub off, to get sore after two days. Periodically the guy would offer the elephant a treat and she would refuse. She refused it for two days. At the end of the two days, she finally accepted the treat. That is when the guy finally stopped the beating. The guy said, I had to do it. This is an environment where you could not allow the elephant to go wild. This is standard procedure in these cases. 'Cause I guess most of them don't take two days but his critics say, it is not training. It is not even behavior modification. This is breaking. Breaking the animal's will, breaking the animal's soul. Something in the animal gave way. Its dignity. Its sense of self or whatever. And [long pause]

my feeling is that is what was done with me when I was a kid. It was
so bad that at the time . . . I don't know what.

Elsa coped with being denied dignity as a child by believing that thinness would take away the limits. When she separated her "skinny"
soul from her fat body, she was protecting her soul from abuse.

Elsa was careful to say that she was not born hating her body. The
hatred was elicited and enforced. The fact that she still considers being
thin the most important goal in her life suggests that the integration
between her body and her soul has yet to occur. Her hatred of fat symbolizes her anger about still being broken: "I associated fat with holding back my dreams. I thought if I was thin I would be this beautiful
person. . . . Being thin meant freedom, appreciation, love, fun." Now
she's not sure that she will ever recover:

> What I ate, what I did, when I moved, when I did not move, every
> little aspect of my physical life was controlled. Somehow I was
> violated as a human being. It broke something in me. [Long silence] I
> don't know if I can get it back together.

MARTHA: *"I didn't have a clue about how to connect with people."*

Martha, a thirty-seven-year-old Jewish lesbian mother, links the onset
of her compulsive eating to emotional abuse she suffered as a child,
abuse that made her feel "disconnected from the world." She never
learned the basic lesson of "connecting with other people" that she believes comes from allowing children to be themselves and trust others
and nurturing them emotionally and physically. Martha describes herself in terms characteristic of abused children, portraying herself as a
lost soul who lacked direction, roots, and a sense of belonging to anyone, including herself.[4] She was almost always alone when she was a
child. She has almost no memories of the time before she was eleven.

Martha grew up in a home in which she was deprived of basic physical and emotional care. There was no touching; she sometimes pre-
tended to be asleep so her father would pick her up and carry her to
bed, providing at least a moment of physical contact. Her father was
rarely home because he worked nights. One of Martha's sisters treated
her as if she were the family's maid. Another was emotionally cruel to
her, keeping Martha from her friends and simultaneously telling Martha that any friends she had were a result of her sister's popularity.

Nor did Martha know how to reach out for attention or friends at
school. When she made her first friend, in eighth grade, and told her

mother about it, her mother said, "Don't get too excited because as high as you will be is as far as you will fall. These people will hurt you." It was a slap in the face, a punch in the chest. Martha cried as she told me the story: "I opened my heart a little and she pulled it down. A lot of emotional abuse and neglect."

The family labeled Martha overly sensitive and teased her incessantly. She cannot remember ever eating a meal with her family when she did not break down and cry because of the teasing. She watched between ten and twelve hours of television each day, even on school days. She knows she was a bright child because she was able to do well in school even though she never studied. There were no books in the house, and she didn't know how to seek them out. She was mildly dyslexic but no one realized it when she was growing up. She was repeatedly told by the members of her family that she was fat and ugly and had no personality. She had no sense of her body size or whether or not she was attractive.

Her mother controlled what Martha and her sisters ate. Even though her sisters were fat and her mother was obese and a compulsive eater, Martha was the one considered to have the biggest problem with food. She was always served last and castigated for eating. Her mother took her to a diet doctor when Martha was eleven and continued to limit her food. Yet her mother also participated in Martha's bingeing. Martha remembers being told by her mother that she could have three cookies each day when she got home from school. Martha would eat three cookies, want more, think about it, and then have more. Then she would struggle to decide whether to get more and usually did, typically stopping after finishing a dozen cookies. Her mother would come home and ask her how many she ate. Martha would lie and say three. Her mother never questioned this openly, although she was the one who filled the cookie jar every day. Although Martha was obviously compulsively eating and lying, no one said anything.

Eating compulsively was how Martha comforted herself from the pain of not feeling connected to any person or to the rest of the world. Bingeing calmed her, leaving her feeling drugged and dazed. When I asked her if she thinks she ate compulsively out of fear of her feelings, she said it wasn't as if she had feelings and then ate to get rid of them. That would assume she had feelings to begin with. That would assume some connection. She ate from disconnection. No specific feelings triggered eating. Simply *being* triggered her desire to eat. She ate, felt numb, and watched television. And no one seemed to care.

CAROLYN: *"Sweets just seemed to be happy food. I thought if I ate them I would get happy."*

Carolyn is a thirty-one-year-old heterosexual African-American woman who grew up in a middle-class family in New York City. She understands her eating problems to have begun when she was six years old when she first remembers "turning to food for things." At the time, she didn't know why she frequently ate whatever she could find. As she understands it now, she began to binge in response to the physical and emotional tension in her family. Her father beat her mother and punished her emotionally, especially if she did anything without his permission. He never allowed her out of the house without him and falsely accused her of having affairs, although he flaunted his adultery, including affairs with relatives. He routinely stalked her, claiming her time as his. If, for example, he called home while she was going to the mailbox and could not hear the phone, he would drive an hour and a half from his workplace to accuse her of having affairs.

Carolyn's father was very strict with the children, and although her mother objected, she could not defend them without being abused. Carolyn's mother "was taking her life into her hands" when she defied him. Even taking her children out trick-or-treating would make him angry. When Carolyn sided with her mother, he beat Carolyn. She remembers her father choking and beating her when she was nine and again at fourteen. She always felt on the edge emotionally, bracing for an explosion:

> I remember my niece asking me one night if I was cold because she thought I was shivering. But I wasn't cold. I was shaking with fear. There was so much tension. My bedroom was right next to theirs so I could hear everything. I would hear him say, "I am getting the gun." I don't even know if he had a gun.

When she was about six, Carolyn began to binge. It was an immediate source of comfort that she couldn't get anywhere else; as is typical of battered mothers, Carolyn's mother was robbed of the vital energy she needed to care for herself and her children. Carolyn ate big portions at meals with her family, then ate secretly too. Eating calmed her, which is why, she says, "I refer to it now as a drug because it numbed me out." Music offered another powerful escape. When it was turned up very loud, it seemed as if nothing else were happening in her world. She could stay up in her room for hours at a time and listen to music, buffered from her violent environment — an especially valuable escape since her father often would not allow her to leave the house.

She could listen to music and eat sweets on her own, without having to rely on anyone else.

If Carolyn didn't have her allowance money, she would go into her mother's purse and take the money to buy food for a binge. She felt as if she were stealing hundreds of dollars and told herself she would pay it back. Despite her guilt, she felt desperate for the food, her "drug."

When Carolyn first began to binge, she believed it was normal. Like many girls who binge when they are very young, she didn't really think about whether anyone else did it. In her mind, it was simply something she did. But as she grew older, she became self-conscious about her weight and learned that her mother didn't like her chunky size. Carolyn knew better than to confess about her binges. Guilt about stealing the money coupled with her fear of eating a lot stopped her from talking about her bingeing with anyone. By keeping her secret, she protected herself from her mother's judgments. Thus Carolyn's coping mechanism remained hidden from view; while it wrapped her in guilt, it nevertheless soothed her.

Recently, Carolyn realized that she liked sweets, especially birthday cakes, so much because they symbolized family harmony and relaxation. Her mother liked to bake, and Carolyn associated sweets with being happy. Birthday cakes were the centerpiece of her childhood. She lived for family birthdays—or rather for the cakes, which in her mind stood for family happiness and peace. The candle-lighting ritual at a birthday party was the one occasion when the family wasn't arguing: "Sweets just seemed to be happy food. I thought if I ate them I would get happy. It seemed so simple." Carolyn's turning to food for comfort was logical since eating was a positive and celebrated part of her childhood. Carolyn waited for the family celebrations, hoping the tension would disappear.

When she was ten years old, she ran away from home with her twelve-year-old sister. She continued to run away until she was sixteen and left for college. She and her sister went to stay at friends' houses in a neighboring town for days and weeks at a time. Once she moved away from home, her bingeing and her appetite subsided. When Carolyn's mother left her father, Carolyn began to live with her mother again. Her problems with food were minimal until she began to diet, pressured by her mother, her boyfriend, and her friends to be thin.

NICOLE: *"Eating was the cave, barrier, boundary, safety, and the buffer."*

Nicole is a forty-one-year-old lesbian of African-American, Cherokee, and white heritage who used food to cope with racism and emotional

and physical abuse. As a young child, Nicole was physically and emotionally abused by her mother, who confined Nicole to the house for
extended periods of time—continuing through her adolescence and
late teens—deliberately tried to kill her, beat her frequently, and forced
Nicole to keep this abuse a secret. Nicole's father did not intervene in
what, as an adult, Nicole has begun to label "torture." Nicole's
mother tried to beat out of Nicole anything that suggested that she was
separate from her mother. Retrospectively, Nicole believes that when
her mother beat her, "she was trying to kill the bad parts of herself."
Her mother had internalized many racist assumptions about black
women and tried to pass them on to Nicole through her judgments
about her hair, skin, and language. Nicole's mother despised anything
that wasn't "white"—curly hair, dark skin, "improper" English.
Nicole bore the brunt of her mother's self-hatred.

When she was a young child, Nicole binged because it made her
"real self disappear," so that no one could find her. Many survivors of
sexual abuse describe a similar splitting process. Whenever she was
physically or verbally attacked at school or by her mother, she would
"disappear":

> I hid my real self inside, very deep inside of a cave or a molecule or a
> cell. That is where I went. Another part of me that was sort of split
> off at the same time was the part that you would see. . . . Eating was
> the cave, barrier, boundary, safety, and the buffer. . . . [The cave was]
> like in science-fiction type stories where there are whole civilizations
> way under the earth. There was a room way under the cave that was
> all stone.

She described this safe place inside her body as filled with huge bal-
loons made of giant globules of fat in cellophane. When she ate she felt
as if she could hide in this room. Now she understands that she escaped into this cave because, deep down, she knew that her mother
was trying to kill her. Nicole embodied a sexual female self that her
mother wanted to destroy.

Bingeing also gave Nicole a way to occupy her time when she was
alone, even though it meant being scolded for being fat. Beginning
when Nicole was three years old, her mother ridiculed her about her
weight and tried to shame her into dieting. Nicole was taken to the
pediatrician routinely to be weighed and given diet pills; these trips humiliated her. While being told she shouldn't eat, Nicole watched her
mother prepare huge meals and learned that eating was an important
family ritual. After school, Nicole was alone for many hours; her parents worked and she was never allowed to play with anyone. She felt
lost and abandoned and did not know what to do with herself, so she

spent the afternoons hunting down and eating the sweets her mother
had hidden from her. Even though she risked her mother's anger, the
ritual of finding the food was like a game: "It was as fun as an Easter
egg hunt to find what new place she had found to hide the food."
While it buffered her loneliness and sadness, the food also gave her a
connection to her mother. Although Nicole and her mother never
talked about this ritual, it was their shared secret since her mother continued to hide food and Nicole continued to search for it and eat it.

Nicole also binged at school to cope with her isolation and empti-
ness. She was sent to private schools and a church in which she was
often the only African-American child, and none of the neighborhood
black or white children went to the schools or church she attended.
She was transferred to a different school almost every year. Abused at
home and racially isolated at school, Nicole had no place to turn. Children of color from troubled families are in double jeopardy, for in addition to suffering the pain inflicted by their families, they have no refuge from racism.

In response to isolation, Nicole binged. Her fifth-grade teacher told
her mother that Nicole ate the extra food from all of the other children's lunches; they gave her what they didn't want and she ate it.
Nicole explains, "I was not getting what I needed to survive [emotion-
ally]. Being tortured. I was being tortured slowly but surely, methodi-
cally. It was all undercover and hidden." Nicole ate whatever was
available, including the hidden cookies and the food her classmates
gave her, often without really thinking about it. Bingeing was more of
an impulse than an action she controlled. She didn't feel guilty about it
except that she knew her mother would be angry. When she was very
young, she didn't associate bingeing with getting fat: "It is more like
the way a dog eats. The way dogs eat out of the garbage. If it is available, they eat it."

Heterosexism

While compulsory heterosexuality influences all women's emerging
sense of themselves, women who link heterosexism directly to their
eating problems tend to be those who acted on their sexual feelings for
other women when they were very young. Their isolation, lack of
knowledge of lesbian communities, and economic and emotional dependence on heterosexual adults explains why coming out as a lesbian
as a child or a teenager may be much more traumatic than coming out
during adulthood.[5] One-third of all suicides of young people are gay-
related; young gay men and lesbians typically shoulder feelings of exclusion alone.[6] The experiences related to me by the women I inter-

viewed illuminate how eating problems emerge as a way of coping with the isolation, confusion, and loneliness of growing up in contexts in which their sexual identities are not embraced.[7]

JACKIE: *"Maybe I could be a more successful heterosexual if I were skinnier."*

Jackie is a twenty-eight-year-old white lesbian who began to worry about her weight during puberty and was bulimic as a teenager. She was always a chubby child, built more like her football-playing father than her slender mother. When puberty began, her parents began to worry that she wasn't going to lose the fat; her mother told her to diet and gave her tips on how to count calories. Soon after, Jackie began to binge, partly because dieting made her hungry. When her mother saw that Jackie was having trouble dieting, she taught Jackie how to throw up, a tactic her mother used occasionally when "she blew her diet." It was a way a woman could eat without having to pay for it, her mother explained. Unbeknownst to her mother, Jackie soon began to binge and throw up daily, a process that continued for two years.

Like many women, Jackie became bulimic after she began to diet, a sequence that suggests that eating problems are partly a physiological response to denial of food.[8] Throwing up was a quick method of compensating for having binged. The fact that Jackie was chunky as a child made her vulnerable to being told that she had to diet. Dieting, in turn, made her vulnerable to bingeing and purging. Without prejudice against fat, she might well have avoided developing these eating habits.

Once she was caught in this cycle, her emerging confusion about her sexual identity contributed to her inability to break the pattern for three years. By the time she was fifteen years old, "I was not being a social, effective heterosexual kid and could not identify in that way, could not imagine being somebody's girlfriend. I just didn't fit that mold." Jackie felt a dissonance between excelling athletically and academically and failing to "fit into the social, sexual scene." During junior high, she says, "kids at school quit saying overt things about weight. Kids don't just go 'hey fatso' any more. It is much more subtle than that. It starts becoming really sophisticated."

Jackie began to notice differences and schisms between friendship networks. One group was made up of the female athletes, many of whom were lesbian (closeted) and most of whom did not diet. Another friendship group consisted of heterosexual girls who dieted, went to the shopping mall, and talked about boys. Dieting appeared to Jackie to be an integral aspect of being a heterosexual girl:

There is this pattern. It seems all the girls were going over to each others' houses and making a batch of cookies and talking about going to the mall. And saying "oh, I am so fat, so fat," even though they were really skinny. And then going to the mall and talking about clothes. This weird kind of torturing each other, but also doing this bonding stuff.

As an athlete, Jackie wasn't part of this group, and she thought that being fat was the reason she was socially inhibited. "Maybe I could be a more successful heterosexual if I were skinnier," she mused. Explaining her confusion about her sexuality, Jackie says, "I was at that age where other people in my peer group were evolving a sexual identity and I wasn't. Or I was but I didn't have that data accessible." Jackie dieted during the day, often skipping breakfast. By night she would be starving and sometimes would binge and purge secretly. While bingeing and throwing up didn't seem to hurt her physically, dieting robbed her of the energy she needed:

I just had two hundred calories from a protein drink and a chicken thigh in my body. I can definitely remember doing wind sprints at basketball practice and thinking, I am going to pass out.

Despite her confusion about her sexual identity and her discomfort with her weight, Jackie did not dislike her body. While most of the women I interviewed had very negative views of their bodies, Jackie maintained a somewhat positive attitude toward hers, partly because of her athletic abilities. She was well coordinated, and her family, peers, and coaches praised her athletic performances. She wanted the status that goes with being thin but was also critical of this aesthetic. As a teenager, she thought being heterosexual meant looking feminine like her mother and being "some guy's girlfriend." She simply couldn't imagine doing either. Now she understands that she has always been "pretty butch identified," which to her means that her emerging sexual identity was related to having a more masculine body: "I never had a self-image of a woman's body that was curvy and voluptuous with hips and breasts and slender thighs. I am built much more like my father."

The problem was that she didn't have words to describe what was happening to her. She knew she had a female body and that she was supposed to be interested in men, yet she "acted really goofy" around girls. She had no way to identify the feelings she had for girls as crushes. When her mother asked if one of the women on the softball team was lesbian, Jackie flatly denied it. Her adamant response reflected the rigid division she had developed: lesbians were bad, heterosexuality was good. Since the women on the softball team were her friends, then, they couldn't be lesbians. Like many children who face seemingly untenable contradictions, Jackie divided the world into good and bad.[9] She remembers weeping on her bed and asking, "How do I fit into the world?" She wondered if maybe all she needed was a friend. But, as she says now, "What I was really trying to say to myself was, I need to be able to express, to myself, my passion, and I don't know how."

She knows now that dieting, bingeing, and purging were means of dealing with the "enormous tension" she felt about her gender identity and sexuality. By dieting, she could focus on a goal—trying to achieve the "right" size for girls. Yet dieting depleted the energy she needed for the sports she loved, so she would binge and then throw up, an easy way to undo the binge. She continued this pattern secretly throughout high school. The cycle began to subside as she began to acknowledge her lesbian identity. Once she started to channel her passion this way, her confusion about her sexual identity lifted. Although she still didn't like her weight, she stopped trying to play the part of a heterosexual and began to feel more like herself.

MARTHA: *"I touched myself with food because you can't touch me because I am queer."*

Martha, a thirty-seven-year-old working-class Jewish woman, began to eat compulsively when she was eleven years old, the same year she started to get clues about her lesbian identity. As is typical of heterosexism, the most devastating forms of discrimination against her were often neither overt nor identified as prejudice, making it hard for her to know what was causing her pain and isolation. Martha experienced heterosexism not only as hostile comments about lesbians, discrimination, and teasing, but also as the daily indignities of heterosexual socialization. At puberty she was told to wear dresses, stop participating in sports, eat "like a lady," and show interest in boys. In junior high, when many of her female classmates began to go out with boys, Martha began to fantasize about girls, which made her feel utterly alone:

> My memories [from] that period of time [have] a whole lot to do with being very lonely and very isolated. . . . At some point someone said, "Okay, now you have to be a girl." And that means you have to go to the Jewish community center on Sundays. I was not into this at all. I wanted to be riding my bike. I wanted to be out playing. I was not into boys from day one.

Martha remembers going to the Jewish community center and hiding behind the coat rack for four hours until someone picked her up. She believed it was wrong to pretend she wanted to dance with the boys when she had no desire to dance with them.

Confused and ashamed about her lesbian desires, Martha responded by making a split between her fantasy life and the life others could see. Knowing it was not safe to tell people about her sexual feelings for girls, she escaped into a secret fantasy world where she loved girls and they loved her, where she was successful and popular. She knew she couldn't tell anyone her secret and, like others who are forced to hide some aspect of themselves, she blamed herself for the ostracism. Her bad behavior (fantasies and masturbation), she told herself, was the reason she didn't have friends and wasn't loved by her family. Impugning herself was logical since she did not know how to direct her anger against prejudice, and at the time, making a split between her fantasy life and the rest of her existence was an act of self-protection. When she separated her fantasy life from the rest of the world, she also separated herself from her gender. In her fantasies, she made herself a boy because that was the only way she could make sense out of sexual desire for a girl. In order to reconcile her sexual feelings, she had to renounce her gender, which increased her feeling of being disconnected from her female body. Like many women, Martha had no sense of herself as connected to her body. When I asked her whether she saw herself as fat when she was growing up, she said, "I didn't see myself as fat. I didn't see myself. I wasn't there. I get so sad about that because I missed so much."

Bingeing was a way to cope with her confusion and the anger she had turned inward. When Martha was eleven she began to come home after school each day and binge, and she continued until she left for college. She would go to the refrigerator and break off pieces of cream cheese and eat them. Bingeing was a way to drug herself that made being alone tolerable and was compensation for not getting physical affection from her family or from girls she liked: "I touched myself with food because you can't touch me because I am queer and I am not getting touched. It begins to be self-fulfilling."

Like many women, Martha binged to soften painful feelings. It sedated her, lessened her anxiety, and induced sleep. It was how she dealt with the fact that her true personality and values were invisible. Her family automatically made many assumptions about her life and future. It was assumed that she would go to college, in keeping with "the whole Jewish ethic of education." It was assumed that she would be heterosexual, that "some button was supposed to go off and then I should deal with boys." Feeling that she was not conforming in any of the ways expected of her, Martha ate constantly. She would come home from school to an empty house and feel desperately alone. Having literally no concept of how to make contact with people, she binged because it was the only thing she knew how to do. Bingeing was just another "bad wrong thing" she did: "Bingeing was like masturbating before I went to sleep." Despite feeling this way, she continued to turn to food, unaware of any alternatives.

When Martha left for college, she met other lesbian women, which allowed her to begin to acknowledge her feelings openly, but heterosexism continued to plague her. She and a college classmate fell in love, but when this woman's father discovered their relationship, he forced his daughter to withdraw from school. When others discovered why this woman could not come back to school, Martha's lesbian identity was revealed. The school administration responded by segregating the women they believed were lesbians into one dorm. Martha felt powerless and guilty, thinking that it was ultimately her fault that her friend couldn't return to school. She continued to binge and began to smoke marijuana, becoming heavier and lonelier than she had ever been. It wasn't until she met women who were comfortable with their lesbian identities that she began to mend the split between her fantasy world (where she could be a lesbian) and the world where she had to hide her sexual identity. As the mending proceeded, her bingeing began to subside.

Poverty

Poverty is another injustice that may make women vulnerable to developing eating problems. The combination of coping with an impersonal, bureaucratic welfare system, staying healthy despite inadequate or nonexistent health care, and paying for child care on a limited income are among the many stresses poverty causes. All women run the risk of being sexually harassed in the workplace, and few escape having to do more than their share of the work at home, but poor women, especially those with children, face many additional stresses that may result in chronic depression, exhaustion, and loneliness.[10] The founder of the National Black Women's Health Project, Byllye Avery, explains one African-American woman's reason for eating compulsively. The woman told Avery:

> I work for General Electric making batteries, and, from the stuff they suit me up in, I know it's killing me. My home life is not working. My old man is an alcoholic. My kid's got babies. Things are not well with me. And one thing I know I can do when I come home is cook me a pot of food and sit down in front of the TV and eat it. And you

can't take that away from me until you're ready to give me something in its place.[11]

For this woman and many others, bingeing is a quick, accessible, and immediately satisfying way of coping with the daily stress of conditions she cannot control. The role of poverty in eating problems shows the damage of portraying them as maladies of upper-class adolescents and underscores how class and race inequalities affect women's eating patterns.

YOLANDA: *"Food doesn't insult you or hurt your feelings."*

One common dimension in the stories of the women I interviewed is that they initially turned to food as a response to lack of power. Yolanda, a black Cape Verdean woman, attributed her compulsive eating, which began when she was twenty-seven, directly to stress caused by poverty. She remembers first eating to fill emotional needs when she was pregnant with her first son and was having difficulties with her husband. After her son was born, she remembers "feeling ugly and out of place" for the first time in her life. One of her friends told her that her stock went down 20 percent since she had had a child. After the birth of her second son, her husband began to abuse her physically while encouraging her to drink and take drugs with him. After many ugly fights, she realized she was "slipping down with him" and felt horrified that her children had seen him beating her: "I didn't want that to happen to them, the way I had grown up. I started fighting back. My kids gave me a lot of strength."

Although she felt sure about her decision to leave him, she was ashamed about the failed marriage and overwhelmed by the demands of raising two children alone. Before she had left Boston to join her husband in the Dominican Republic, she had always had a job that paid well. When she returned to Boston alone with her children, she had trouble finding work that would cover her expenses, including child-care costs:

> I used to walk to the A & P and put the bags on the stroller so I wouldn't have to spend three dollars for someone to drive me home. I had six bags. . . . I remember being on the street, in the snow, in the rain, in the dark with two small kids trying to take the bus down to my mother's house so she could take care of them.

Like many women with small children, Yolanda was forced to make the "choice" between going on welfare and leaving her children alone while she worked. On welfare, she tried to support herself and her children on $539 a month—a truly meager amount for a family of three in the late 1980s. She desperately wanted to go to college, having been a good student and a campus leader in high school. When she applied to college before her children were born, she had been accepted in several places, but only a college she had never heard of in Arkansas had offered financial aid. She didn't know any black people in Arkansas, and, having never been there herself, decided against it. After she returned from the Dominican Republic, she launched a search for a university in the Boston area that would help her financially. Meanwhile, she began to binge in the evenings after putting her children to bed. Eating was something she could do alone. It calmed her, helped her deal with loneliness, and made her feel safe:

> I would eat whole meals. Not like a snack. I mean steak with rice and potatoes. I would eat real fast. I would eat to the point where my stomach hurt. I could eat two plates of food in less time than it would take someone to eat one. Then afterwards I'd feel miserable, asking why did I eat that? Ten minutes later I'd be looking for something sweet to top it off.

Even when money was especially low, she could still binge on inexpensive food; she ate three boxes of macaroni and cheese when nothing else was available. In the following three years she gained seventy pounds.

Eating was a temporary release from financial pressures. Stretching her money through the month was impossible:

> You are always doing this rotating. . . . I'd get backed up with my gas bill so I'd have to play catch up. . . . My son joined a baseball team and that cost twenty dollars. My other son had a birthday and I made him a cake. What really gets me is even if I'd get all my bills paid, I'd need money every day, even if it is for a cup of coffee or a package of cigarettes. I never really have that money aside. So I'd end up borrowing ten dollars. . . . Me and my girlfriends will borrow ten dollars back and forth. It might go around the three of us twice in a month.

Bingeing at night soothed her and, since she could not afford to hire someone to watch the children and go out, it was recreation.

Yolanda's bingeing also was rooted in what she calls the "emotional damage" she suffered as a child as a result of the violence she witnessed. For Yolanda as for many survivors of trauma, the psychological consequences weren't clear until many years later. Yolanda's father was shot in the back by a police officer when she was three years old. At the time, her family was denied information about the details surrounding his death. Her mother hired a lawyer, but "everything got screwed up somehow and they ended up transferring the cop to California. So I never knew my father." She was left fatherless and haunted by not knowing more about how and why he died.[12] Her alcoholic stepfather beat her mother, who slept with a baseball bat to protect herself. Yolanda remembers her stepfather walking around the house bleeding from his head after her mother finally fought back. One way she coped with the violence was to leave her body:

> It is like being in a fog. Like I was not really there. I was kind of invisible. . . . It seemed like I was looking at stuff but I wasn't really there. . . . It was like it wasn't really me. I wasn't part of what was going on.

She had told herself that she "wasn't going to let anything drive me crazy. In order not to do that effectively, I had to not be there."

By contrast, when she had to raise her two children alone, she resided fully in her body for the first time in her life. When I asked her why she came into her body then, she said, "It was probably about having to deal with everything all by myself." Her adult body became her only refuge:

> I am here [in my body] because there is nowhere else for me to go. Where am I going to go? This is all I got. . . . That probably contributes to putting on so much weight 'cause staying in your body, in your home, in yourself, you don't go out. You aren't around other people. . . . You hide and as long as you hide you don't have to face . . . nobody can see you eat. You are safe.

By numbing painful emotions, bingeing allowed Yolanda to remain in her body and cope with the constraints thrust upon her. When she was eating, Yolanda relaxed for the moment. Bingeing was a logical solution not only because it was cheap and easy but also because she had grown up amid positive messages about eating. In her family, eating was a joyful act:

> The only way my stepfather knew how to love was through food. This lesson is a hard one to break. How do you substitute something that makes you feel better whenever you feel bad? Food doesn't insult you or hurt your feelings. People do.

In adulthood, however, eating became a double-edged sword. While eating comforted her, it also caused her to gain weight. Struggling emotionally and financially, Yolanda went underground as her weight gain exacerbated her feelings that she had no right to be seen. She stopped going on dates, wearing makeup, dressing on mornings she didn't have classes or work. Sometimes she took long naps when her kids were in school. As another mother said about coping with mothering and poverty:

> I ain't gonna worry myself about everything that happens—you
> crazy? I'd be dead from worryin' if I did that or be in the nut-house,
> either one. No, not me. Might sound funny but know what I do
> when I got trouble? I get in the bed and go to sleep. Now I know
> that doesn't solve my problem but it is better than worryin' till you
> get yourself crazy like all these other mothers. I will admit I been
> sleepin' too much in the daytime, though, and I know that ain't good
> for me—can't get anything done that way, your house work,
> shopping. But it's better'n always hollerin' or beatin' up the kids. It's
> better than takin' dope and pills, that's for sure.[13]

Sleeping and bingeing took the edge off Yolanda's worries. These self-conscious coping strategies were far better than many others she could have adopted. Her oldest brother had recently been suspended for the third time from the fire department for drinking. Another brother was in a shelter for people addicted to heroin and other drugs. For Yolanda, compulsive eating was the least destructive way of coping. She saw it as more socially acceptable than getting drunk, partly because "I didn't hurt anyone but myself in the process."

Immigration and Acculturation

The stresses of acculturation may also lead to eating problems. Acculturation is the lengthy and complex process by which people modify their cultural practices as they adjust to a new culture. It is influenced by political, social, religious, economic, and historical forces. The extent to which acculturation is destructive is partly a function of the degree to which a distinct racial, cultural, or ethnic group is forced to take on the values of the more dominant group through assimilation. Adrienne Rich describes a range of characteristic attempts to assimilate:

> Change your name, your accent, your nose; straighten or dye your
> hair; stay in the closet; pretend the Pilgrims were your fathers;
> become baptized as a christian; wear dangerously high heels, and
> starve yourself to look young, thin, and feminine; don't gesture with
> your hands; value elite European culture above all others; laugh at
> jokes about your own people; don't make trouble; defer to white
> men; smile when they take your picture; be ashamed of who you are.
> To assimilate means to give up not only your history but your body,
> to try to adopt an alien appearance because your own is not good
> enough, to fear naming yourself lest name be twisted into label.[14]

Some degree of assimilation is demanded of all people in the United States who are not members of the dominant group—which is white, Christian, able-bodied, heterosexual, wealthy, and male. This is true whether they immigrate to the United States or are born here. The assimilation required of immigrants whose cultures of origin are similar to the dominant culture, however, has been far less destructive than that of immigrants who come involuntarily, who speak languages other than English, and who enter the United States in poverty.[15] For the latter groups, adopting Anglo cultural values has been not voluntary but, to some degree, necessary for survival.[16] As psychologists Durhane Wong-Rieger and Diana Quintana explain:

> In theory, the American "melting pot" implies acculturation by both new and host members; in reality, minorities, because of their small numbers, low status, lack of power and visibility, are expected to conform to the majority.[17]

Maintaining cultural ties and traditions amid pressures to assimilate is an intricate effort that has remained the centerpiece of many immigrants' lives, often for several generations.

Gender also influences the social and psychological consequences of immigration. The psychological reactions to immigration are often analogous to those associated with other types of major loss.[18] Oliva Espin writes:

> Immigration or any other form of separation from cultural roots involves a process of grieving. Women seem to be affected by this process in a manner that is different from that of men. Successful adaptation after immigration involves resolution of feelings of loss, the development of decision making skills, ego strength, and the ability to tolerate ambiguities, including sex-role ambiguities.[19]

Women may be denied power as mothers and wives that was afforded to them in their native countries. Isolation and new demands result from being separated from their extended families. They may lose confidence about being able to provide for their family's safety and be anxious about acceptance. Conflicts between spouses or between parents and daughters as a result of new gender expectations are a frequent stress for immigrant women.[20] Latina, African-Caribbean, and Asian immigrant women endure job-related stresses—including sexual harassment, dead-end jobs, and poor or no benefits—familiar to many women in the labor market. As a result of racism, they also face higher unemployment and underemployment than white immigrant women do.[21] These various stresses suggest why women may become bulimic or anorexic as methods of coping.[22]

Three of the eighteen women I interviewed immigrated to the United States, but they came under very different circumstances. Julianna, the Dominican woman, and Gilda, who partially grew up in North Africa, came from families who were forced to leave their native countries as a result of political or religious persecution. Elsa, who is Argentinean, immigrated to the United States voluntarily when she was in her thirties. Immigrating enabled her to gain the control over her life that was denied her in Argentina, which helped her begin to deal with her eating problems. Gilda, who immigrated when she was five years old, identified her compulsive eating as a response to being raped. This trauma and her response to it interrupted her traditional cultural eating patterns. The process of acculturation deeply influenced her response to the rape and her process of turning to food for comfort (see chapter 3). The three women's experiences make clear that acculturation, unlike heterosexism, sexual abuse, and emotional abuse, is not uniformly detrimental to a woman's sense of her body and to her eating patterns. Awareness of the possible tensions of acculturation can, however, illuminate the meaning of eating problems for immigrant women.

JULIANNA: *"I could never explain hot dogs to my mom."*

Julianna, who immigrated to the United States from the Dominican Republic, associates her eating problems with the stresses of acculturation. A twenty-four-year-old heterosexual Latina who was raised by her grandmother in a small town in the Dominican Republic, she came to the United States when she was sixteen. When she was three, her parents fled the Dominican Republic to escape death threats related to her father's opposition to the dictatorship. They came to the United States without papers, leaving their daughter and younger son behind with the children's grandmother.

Unlike many of the women I interviewed, Julianna liked her body when she was growing up and was not subjected to diets or diet pills. In the Dominican Republic, thinness was not considered a necessary attribute for female beauty. In fact, if Julianna had any problem with food as a child, it was not wanting to eat all the food her grandmother prepared. Her grandmother told her that she couldn't get up from the table until she ate. Julianna was very straightforward and stubborn and would sit at the table for three, four, or five hours, protesting. With this refusal, Julianna exerted her will against her grandmother's protective child-rearing practices: "There are so many things about Spanish culture that don't let people be themselves. Especially when you are a woman. Little girls don't do this. Little girls don't do that."

Julianna's refusal to eat was a minor issue, however, and it did not lead to any real problems.

When she joined her parents in the United States, Julianna's relationship to food and her body changed dramatically as she began to diet and became bulimic. Separated from her parents since she was a toddler, she had grieved their absence constantly: "I felt such a crush inside of me because I could never see their faces." Yet she had not wanted to leave the Dominican Republic or her grandmother. She was not consulted about her parents' decision that she would join them in the United States, and she wondered if she had become too much work for her grandmother.[23] As an adult she understands, intellectually, the reason for her parents' exile—they had been forced to "choose" between dying and watching their children grow up from a great distance—but she was also angry that they had left the Dominican Republic without her.

She had to cope with learning English among native English speakers, who were impatient and teased her. She had come from a country where she was in the majority, and she had been taught not to be prejudiced. In the United States, she felt out of place:[24]

> I didn't speak the language and couldn't make any friends. And
> everyone lives so far away. Everybody looked so rude when I came
> here. I was used to when you meet a girl you kiss [her] on the cheek.
> When you say goodbye you kiss [her] mother goodbye on the cheek
> too.

Julianna began to eat more and eat different kinds of food than she had in the Dominican Republic. In her native country she had always eaten meals with her relatives; eating at school was simply not done. In the United States she ate breakfast with her family and then again at school with classmates who would tease her if she did not do so. At lunchtime she ate a big meal at home, in part because she could not get used to "American" food: "Hamburgers I didn't like. Pizzas! I thought that was disgusting. Hot dogs. I could never explain hot dogs to my mom." After school she came home to an empty house since both of her parents worked. She no longer had the strict schedule her grandmother had imposed on her nor her grandmother's company. She had no homework to occupy her since she was academically advanced in comparison to the students at school. Whereas in the Dominican Republic people shopped for fresh food every day and only ate during meals, in the United States the refrigerator was full of food and people snacked constantly. Bingeing became her distraction and her pleasure.

The confusion caused by conflicting cultural standards weakened

Julianna's body image. She had a perfect body by Dominican standards, what her friends called a "guitar body." Dominican men

> liked beautiful legs and beautiful behinds. . . . Big and fat. Something
> you could notice from far away. . . . Women are not supposed to be
> skinny. Instead of bones, they are supposed to have some flesh. Men
> like that.

In the United States Julianna quickly learned that being thin was crucial for women, that the

> value on appearance is so deeply ingrained in Anglo culture that it
> would be very hard to explain another way of seeing things. Many
> Hispanics, on the other hand, have been raised to understand beauty
> in a deeper way. That, in fact, is one of the strengths of Hispanic
> culture.

Julianna began to question her body size. Although she was slim,
she began to think her body was fat. As Cynthia Bulik writes:

> Given that all cultures do not emphasize slimness to the extent that
> American culture does, the discrepancy between the body of the
> immigrant and the American ideal can serve to increase the sense of
> alienation and not belonging to the new society.[25]

When a close female family friend and classmates told Julianna to diet,
she accepted their judgments. Her brother who grew up in the United
States called her fat—although she was not—and told her to diet. Even
her brother who had just immigrated quickly adopted the emphasis on
thinness and began to tease Julianna. She fasted for entire days and
eventually became so hungry that she binged. Eating that had begun as
a way to cope with loneliness, boredom, and homesickness became
coupled with eating that was a physiological response to fasting. She
began to get up in the middle of the night to watch television and
binge.
   Julianna's change in eating patterns also was a reaction to her father's alcoholism. She was angry that he drank so much; when he
didn't change, she started to refuse to eat traditional Dominican
meals: "Sometimes I wouldn't eat [as a way] to hurt my father. I
wouldn't eat in front of him. Morning, afternoon, and night I would
make him suffer. I was mad at him because of his drinking." While she
was refusing to eat with her family, she binged on junk food secretly.
She ate so much that her "stomach couldn't take it" and then she
threw up.[26] Her loneliness and isolation are characteristic of many
adult children of alcoholics, and in her case they were exacerbated by
the isolation of a recent immigrant. She says, "I thought I was going

crazy 'cause I didn't have anyone to talk to." The stigma of alcoholism, like the secrecy associated with sexual abuse, caused her to cope with her anger and pain alone and led her to blame herself when she couldn't make her father quit drinking. But stuffing herself upset her too: "I was doing something against my will. I was eating and I was full. My system didn't want to take it. Didn't want to accept it."

When Julianna began to regain the power she had lost by immigrating to the United States—as she learned English, made friends, learned about alcoholism, and met other women with eating problems—her eating problems subsided. To protect herself from her father's alcoholism, she began to pull away from her family, although this meant that she was diminishing her connection to Dominican culture. Her gestures of independence angered her family, and they were upset by her stepping out of traditional Latina sex roles. Her refusal to eat with the family, originally a way to punish her father, was a symptom not only of her eating problems but also of cultural conflicts. Going to college empowered her, but she still felt she had to distance herself from her family and cultural ties.

The challenges of Julianna's emerging bicultural identity were evident in her changing relationship to language. Oliva Espin writes that it is important to address the

> affective and cognitive implications of bilingualism and language . . .
> [because] even for those Latinas who are fluent in English, or who
> have lost fluency in the use of their first language, Spanish remains
> the language of emotions because it was in Spanish that affective
> meanings were originally encoded.[27]

At the end of the interview, I asked Julianna how the interview might have been different had it been in Spanish. She emphatically said it would have been harder, which baffled me at first. I had assumed that since her first language was Spanish and the interview involved personal issues and memories about a time in her life when she thought and felt exclusively in Spanish, she would have found speaking in English restrictive. But in Julianna's mind, English is a more liberal language than Spanish, a language she would dare to use when talking about eating problems, her anger toward her father, and her struggle for independence. She said that speaking English "makes you feel liberal. It is like a synonym: liberal and independent and women's rights and English. That is the way I think about it." Spanish is the language she spoke before she

> learned how to speak for myself. . . . Spanish is the language I grew
> up with, and I never talked when I was growing up. . . . It is like I

have two personalities, one in Spanish and one in English. When I
speak in English, I think in English and I am American. When I come
to my home, I speak Spanish.

Oliva Espin writes that

using the second language can act as a facilitator for the emergence
and discussion of certain topics. Some of these may be taboo topics
or words in Spanish while others may refer to the new components
of the self acquired through the process of acculturation after English
became the primary or most used language.[28]

Perhaps the most convincing evidence that Julianna's eating problems
were symptoms of the strain of acculturation is her unequivocal use of
English when she thinks and talks about them.

Psychic Violence and Physical Violations

The term "eating problem," while it is better than "eating disorder," is
still a misnomer. In fact, women's changed eating patterns more often
begin as solutions to problems than as problems themselves. Their narratives also illuminate ways trauma can be inflicted. While many
women link eating problems to physical intrusions, others relate them
to the psychic invasions of heterosexism, poverty, the stress of acculturation, racism, and emotional abuse. A combination of physical and
psychic assaults leaves many women vulnerable to bingeing, purging,
and dieting.[29]

Psychic abuse is sometimes more difficult to identify than physical
assault, yet the effects can be as devastating to one's sense of self. It is
easy for a woman to deny or to minimize the damage done by psychic
abuse—or by physical assaults that leave marks. Many rationalize that
"someone else's pain is far worse than mine," forsaking their right to
express or identify pain. Both separating and ranking psychic and
physical violence trivialize the consequences of trauma.

An integrated view of trauma rests on recognizing how psychic and
physical violence are often intertwined. The Puerto Rican activist and
psychologist Elba Crespo writes:

The violence of racism need not be a direct physical attack. For
example, consider the young man who walks around in a tee-shirt
with the printed message "Speak English or Die." The message is
clear: If you dare to be different you deserve to be the victim of
violence. This threat of violence, and its potential effect of keeping
people of color quiet, is not different from the fear and powerlessness
experienced by women who have been victimized by verbal abuse.

The threat of physical injury and/or death is a powerful tool of repression and control.[30]

An expansive perspective rejects false dichotomies between psychic and physical violence. Crespo explains:

> If we are to be successful, we must recognize how the entire experience of violence fits into the life experiences of women of color, and not just violence in [their homes]. . . . For example, let's assume that a woman has decided to leave [her] abuser. She is poor, African-American and has three children. While the violence . . . may have ended, she must still deal with discrimination in her search for housing and employment, in fighting the stereotypes of the single black mother and other forms of discrimination. She will still experience racism. Consider the parallels to the work that we do to address physical and emotional violence. If the batterer's physical abuse has ceased but the verbal and emotional abuse continues, we would not consider that a woman has escaped violence in her life. Why then would we assume that if a woman of color ends the physical violence in her home that she has ended violence in her life?[31]

Finally, recognizing both psychic and physical assaults helps avoid the historical tendency to identify the body and the mind as somehow disconnected entities. A violation of emotional or intellectual capacities is felt in the body, and the response to it is also experienced in a bodily way. Similarly, a woman who is physically abused uses her mind to protect herself. The link between the body and the mind is also evident in the close relationship between a woman's psychological and physical boundaries. Often, when a woman loses an accurate sense of her body size and shape, this indicates that her psychological boundaries have been compromised as well.[32] The effectiveness of eating problems as coping devices lies in their versatility—in their ability to soothe the mind and the body simultaneously.

5   A Thousand Hungers

Who hurt you so,
My dear?
Who, long ago
When you were very young,
Did, said, became, was . . . something that you did not know
Beauty could ever do, say, be, become? —
So that your brown eyes filled
With tears they never, not to this day, have shed . . .
Not because one more boy stood hurt by life,
No: because something deathless had dropped dead —
An ugly, an indecent thing to do —
So that you stood and stared, with open mouth in which the tongue
Froze slowly backward toward its root,
As if it would not speak again, too badly stung
By memories thick as wasps about a nest invaded
To know if or if not you suffered pain.

Edna St. Vincent Millay[1]

Why Food?

The connection between trauma and eating problems raises a key question: Why food? Why do women turn to food rather than some other way of coping? A common thread running through the stories of the women I interviewed is the power of food to buffer pain. Women across race, class, and sexuality began to diet or to binge to help them numb difficult emotions—rage, anger, loneliness, anxiety, fear. Like liquor, bingeing sedates, lessens anxiety, and induces sleep.[2] Describing the effects of bingeing, the women said it "put me back to sleep after a nightmare," "made me numb out," "helped me stuff back emotions." Eating "was a break from the stress," a way to "deny all my feelings." Bingeing gave them a high, a feeling of contentment that countered the crying spells, nightmares, and depression that plagued many of them as children and young adults. Bingeing cut them off from uncomfortable and upsetting emotions. The fact that many of the women first began to remember trauma-related dreams after they stopped bingeing suggests that eating large quantities of food, like abusing alcohol, can reduce one's dream state. (Alcohol abuse interrupts dream patterns, reducing the amount of rapid eye movement sleep.)[3]

Although bingeing was the most common way these women numbed emotions, paradoxically, dieting served a similar function, helping them avoid painful feelings by giving them a goal—not eating—to focus on. This concentration, like the focus runners need before a race, distracted them from pain, anger, and confusion. Many initially binged, then learned to use dieting in a similar way as they grew older. They were ostracized or punished for bingeing, were told that an ample appetite is not socially acceptable for females, and were erroneously led to believe that weight gain is a direct function of eating. Had they been taught that a person's weight is influenced by a number of factors—including genetics, types of food eaten, and metabolism—not simply governed by self-control and counting calories, they might have been able to avoid the cycles of weight gain and loss associated with dieting. Instead, they began to diet as a means of focusing their attention on something they could control—a socially acceptable focus beyond their pain.

The anesthetic power of bingeing and dieting makes sense, but why did the women choose food rather than alcohol or other drugs? One reason is that food is available to young girls who don't have the money or mobility to get other drugs. They were searching for a narcotic long before they had access to liquor, prescription drugs, or street drugs: the ages of these women when they were sexually abused ranged from four to twelve; the average age was seven. Other forms of trauma also hit early. A few of the women's earliest memories were of their fathers beating their mothers. Several were victimized emotionally before they were five. Food was the most accessible and socially acceptable drug available. When they began to binge as young girls, they could simply go to the kitchen for food. Those who did not have direct access to food stole money from their mothers' purses, took their classmates' lunches, and hid food for when they needed it. The availability, accessibility, and affordability of food made it their drug of choice.

Eating that began as a simple solution to pain then became a generalized response to stress. While a few of the women began to use other drugs as they grew older, most continued to turn to food. Trepidation about alcohol and illegal drugs kept some focused on food. Those who grew up with an alcoholic parent—or two—learned early the dangers of excessive drinking. Food seemed significantly less dangerous than alcohol, for them and for their children. Bingeing can also be less expensive than drinking.

Using food rather than drugs is partly a function of gender social-ization and women's many responsibilities: you can binge at night and still get up in the morning, get children ready for school, and be clear-headed for college classes and work—without the hangover alcohol would cause. Women can overindulge in food and still do the work most women do: caring for children, driving, cooking, and holding down a job. When one woman's compulsive eating was at its height, she ate breakfast at home, stopped for a snack on her way to work, went to three different cafeterias for lunch, and snacked at her desk throughout the afternoon. Even when her eating had become constant, she was able to hold a job; eating enabled her to go on without falling apart emotionally. While that much food no doubt affected her pro-ductivity, being drunk or hung over would have been far worse.

Women raised in families and communities in which food was a sign of celebration naturally turned to food for comfort, but the pres-sures of assimilation and class expectations eventually denied them this consolation, and many went from bingeing to dieting. Many of the women who initially responded to trauma by purging and dieting were bombarded in childhood with messages that they should diet and be thin. For some, adolescence brought lessons in how to refine dieting techniques; a few were taught by family members how to be bulimic.

Bingeing and dieting are simple coping mechanisms because they are solitary. As children, many of the women were forced to rely on themselves as they reckoned with the loneliness that comes from a be-trayal of trust. Children who are abused by family members have a vested interest in keeping the abuse secret; they often know the abuse is wrong but they are also aware that their families are "all" they have. Periodic fantasies of trading in their families for new ones are just that—fantasies. They know that reporting abuse could divide the fam-ily in possibly irreparable ways and leave them with no family at all. Many girls are programmed by abusers to believe the abuse is their own fault.[4] Almost all of the women I talked with experienced trauma alone and, in many instances, had no choice but to endure isolation; they used methods of coping that maintained their anonymity.

With the knowledge that they could figure out ways to care for themselves, they regained power. A girl might not be able to stop her father from beating her mother, or make the children at school pay attention to her, or return to her native country, or make the welfare department provide decent assistance for women with children, but she *could* treat herself to food late at night, try to lose weight, or throw up food she wished she hadn't eaten. They knew not to tell others about their eating, and they could find ways to do it without getting caught. Those who dieted not only got a sense of control but also were praised for their discipline and willpower.

Some of the women began to eat or to diet to cope with simultaneous physical, psychic, and spiritual losses. Some lost their belief in "god" and in the protection of a benevolent force. Those who were sexually abused lost trust in their caretakers; their bedrooms, homes, and playgrounds no longer felt safe. They also lost a sense of innocence, authenticity, and subjectivity and what Ellen Bass refers to as "the gift of anger."[5] The girls whose mothers were beaten realized that their mothers' ability to protect and support them was limited. The battered mothers' confidence and hopes for the future were slight, and their daughters often lost a sense of possibility for themselves as well. Like the victims of sexual abuse, they too lost the sense of home as a safe place. Running away from home for extended periods of time — as three of the women did — was a telling indicator of being robbed of a refuge.

For those who recognized their lesbian identities when they were young, acknowledging their sexuality meant losing family and friends. Those who came out were beaten by their parents, forbidden to see their lovers, told by their parents that they would rather have a *puta* (whore) than a *pata* (dyke) for a daughter, and persecuted at college by administrators and fellow students. The threatened loss of support was especially frightening to lesbians of color, since their families were their central link to their racial and cultural communities; they risked losing family and community simultaneously.[6]

Moving to the United States ushered in enormous loss as immigrant women were cut off from the friendships, communities, families, rituals, smells, food, and music that they had grown up with.[7] Adjusting to what are often perceived as the cold and distant ways of the United States left them feeling desperately alone, grieving for the comforts of home. While some gained more freedom of movement in the United States, the expectation that they would remain devoted and dedicated to their parents denied them independence and autonomy.

Poverty robs women of confidence and freedom. Poor women often have no car, which restricts their mobility. They can't enroll their children in a soccer league or buy themselves a new shirt without having to scrimp on food. Both small and big financial decisions are difficult when there is no money. And welfare subjects women to bureaucracy and humiliation while robbing them of independence and control.

Some of the women were able to grieve losses and disempowerment when they happened, but for others the grieving was postponed, leaving them overwhelmed and burdened by unfinished business. Financial or emotional demands robbed some of the women of the time and energy they needed to heal. Prolonged drug abuse and the numbed state that accompanies bingeing slowed the grieving process for others. Many of them experienced one trauma right on top of another, giving them little chance to make sense of events or to recover from them. Layering of losses, one right after another, can make someone silent and numb, "too badly stung by memories thick as wasps."[8] Explaining the cumulative effect of successive losses, the journalist Bridgett Davis writes:

> Loss is painful no matter what. But when the loss comes so fast and furious, and in succession as it has in my life, the pain reaches a piercing height, has a menacing spin to it. So little time exists for growing a protective crust over the open wounds caused by one death before another one happened. A deep survival instinct led me, I think, to grow numb after a while.[9]

In times of grief and sadness, food is an immediate companion. When as girls the women began to look for food in the middle of the night, they were searching for something they could count on to keep them company and help them get back to sleep. Metaphorically, their attempts can also be seen as a search for lost innocence. Some hunted all over their houses for sweets their mothers had hidden, searching for love and affection as well as for food. They wrestled with anger, confusion, and betrayal as pain rained down on them with such intensity that bingeing or dieting seemed their only comfort.

Food became a drug of choice for some as a consequence of the amnesia that characteristically follows many types of trauma, both physical and psychic. Most of the survivors of sexual abuse "forgot" the abuse and have only recently begun to retrieve memories of it. Those who endured the pain of heterosexist exclusion sometimes did not remember the details until adulthood. Those who were physically abused or saw others being hurt often did not begin to regain memories until many years later. These gaps in memory left them unable to explain or understand their feelings of shame, fear, depression, and loss. When the feelings or fragments of the memories resurfaced in dreams or when something reminded them of previous events, they could not attach their distress to its cause. This left them feeling out of control and confused. Some recall waking up with nightmares and searching for food; at the time they had no idea what caused the dreams or made them want to eat. Those who described feeling disconnected from the world or out of place at school had little idea at the time why they binged after school each day or purged in order to be able to binge without gaining weight.

Individual amnesia is fueled by what Adrienne Rich calls "historical amnesia," an erasure, glossing over, or distortion of history that occurs when an official version of history—which reflects those in power—is substituted for the actual stories of people's struggles against inequality.[10] Two of the most obvious examples of historical amnesia are romanticized versions of Columbus's arrival in the Caribbean and nostalgic stories of the "taming of the West"—that is, the genocide of Native American people. Historical amnesia robs us of accounts of oppressed peoples' struggles against social injustice and their triumphs, and at the same time romanticizes the oppressors. Historical amnesia tells us that each injustice is an isolated incident rather than part of a larger historical frame. There are myriad repercussions of historical amnesia on individual lives. Among the women I spoke with, the young lesbians knew they were lonely and wished for more friends without knowing how to put a name to the source of their alienation. Historical amnesia has erased the history of lesbians who, despite isolation and loneliness, have survived and even thrived. As a consequence, they didn't understand the politics of their emotions; they did not have the language, memories, or political consciousness to understand what was causing their isolation.

The Latina and African-American girls who attended predominantly white schools knew they felt left out, but it was hard for them to articulate the social injustice behind their pain or to realize that they were not alone, crazy, or too sensitive. Instead, they were left to struggle alone against the historical amnesia evident in the myth that desegregation solved the problems of exclusion and discrimination in education. Situating individual struggle in a larger social reality is even more difficult for those who do not learn survival strategies from their families. Bingeing, dieting, and purging become understandable ways of numbing out amid this confusion.

Although the ability of bingeing and dieting to buffer pain explains how eating problems begin for girls across race, class, sexuality, and religion, the analogy between eating problems and drug use can only be taken so far. While food works like drugs by affecting mood, the dynamics are decidedly different. While use of illicit drugs is typically associated with trying to create a new reality, bingeing and dieting, at least initially, allow a person to cope with an unavoidable reality. Ultimately, this is why eating problems backfire: the ability to continue on can mask tremendous pain over many years. While bingeing, purging, and dieting may have saved them from abusive drinking, this is a mixed blessing because few people detected their problems, limiting the possibility of positive intervention. As Dawn says:

Food is not taken seriously and I guess is not as debilitating as drugs or alcohol. Someone has to hit a pretty severe bottom for it to really show up, for you to lose your house over being a food addict, for you to lose status in this society, whereas alcohol brings you down real quick.

Antonia says it even more emphatically: "Eating disorders, or whatever anybody decides to call them at this point, [are] the most socially acceptable way to self-destruct."

The Progression of Eating Problems

Bingeing and dieting often begin as a sensible response to trauma, but eventually they usually cause problems of their own. Joselyn appropriately characterized them as "coping skills/antiskills," an accurate summation of how many of the women I interviewed described the progression of their eating problems.

Bingeing became a problem partly because, as they grew up, they increasingly internalized the cultural demand for thinness. Those who began to binge when they were only four or five years old were not self-conscious about their eating, nor did they necessarily feel guilty about it. They simply did it. Some were not yet aware of the popular misconception that all people who are fat "got that way" by eating too much, and therefore didn't know they would be blamed if they were big. By the time they were eight or nine years old, however, many had effectively internalized cultural messages about eating and their bodies: that their eating habits were the sole reason for their body size, that bingeing is a sign of lack of willpower and self-discipline, and that they should feel ashamed of having big appetites.

For many, dieting that began as a response to an invasion of their bodily integrity eventually hindered them rather than helped them control what they ate; cycles of bingeing and dieting undermined their confidence that they could control their eating. As a consequence of long-term dieting—which lowers metabolism—some of them found that they could only eat small amounts without gaining weight. Bingeing was a frequent reaction to hunger caused by dieting.

Had they not internalized the cultural ideology, their use of food to cope with childhood trauma might have remained simply that, but once they were familiar with bingeing or dieting, they continued to use these methods when they were faced with later traumas: rape, violent relationships, racist and heterosexist discrimination. Consequently, in addition to the physiological effects of cycles of dieting and bingeing, the women had to deal with the psychological effects of their method of coping. Bingeing, purging, and dieting helped them get by but did little to help them combat the source of their pain or to untangle the reasons behind their actions. In fact, bingeing and dieting often put on hold the emotional work they needed to do. With each painful experience they countered with bingeing or yet another severe diet, more unresolved feelings accumulated. Many of the women have spent years coming to terms with this reality. As Laura says, "It took me a long time to realize that the thing that I turned to for comfort was the thing that would turn on me."

Some of the women characterize their eating problems as addictions that became increasingly worse. A few believe they were born with a partially genetically determined food addiction;[11] Laura is one of them:

> I have the earliest memories of just savoring Twinkies. I was very little. I would go to people's houses and I would end up in the kitchen trying to find those little sprinkles you put on cakes. I just had this very bizarre relationship with food. I learned very quickly that clearing the table as a chore was a good thing to do because I got to eat everybody's leftovers.

By the time she was three years old she was sneaking shots of liquor from a cabinet. Since her nuclear and extended family included people addicted to alcohol and heroin—in addition to those she considers food addicts—she believes that her addiction to alcohol and food was "in my blood" and that it was impossible for her to escape it. Most of the women do not consider their eating problems genetic, but do link them with other family members' abuse of alcohol, illegal drugs, and food. Almost all of the women had at least one parent who was addicted to alcohol or other drugs or had a long-term eating problem; as youngsters, they watched their parents use alcohol, drugs, and food to get through the day.

Some of the women's eating problems eventually became life-threatening—Dawn's, for example. She began to diet, binge, and purge intermittently prior to adolescence, consuming many sweets and carbohydrates. By the end of high school, she was eating all of the sweets in the house, including those in the freezer. Before adolescence she binged with others, but by the end of high school and early adulthood, she no longer let anyone see her eat. In her last binges she would consume massive quantities of food beginning in the early morning and continue until she could eat no more. Then she would throw everything up, and within half an hour or so she would begin to eat again. During the year before she sought treatment, Dawn says,

all of a sudden this feeling would come over me . . . the compulsion
to eat would start at my head and go down through my body. Then I
would just grab my keys and run out of the apartment and run to the
store and shove food in my mouth so that I could continue to eat.

A combination of anorexia, bulimia, and intravenous drug abuse
brought her dangerously close to death in her mid-twenties. She had
begun to use Ipecac, an inexpensive over-the-counter drug that is used
to induce vomiting to counter poisoning:

> Sticking my fingers down my throat was a nice way to puke because
> you don't get all those body shivers. You know when you have a
> fever? Well, taking Ipecac makes you all clammy and disgusting. Then
> you start to dry heave and then food starts coming up. You have no
> control over it. You have convulsions. It is the most horrifying
> experience of my entire life. That is where my bingeing brought me.
> That is how far it progressed. I stopped being able to go to Narcotics
> Anonymous meetings. I was eating a dozen doughnuts and puking.

It was at this point that Dawn sought the inpatient treatment program
that she credits with saving her life.

Rosalee's compulsive eating became progressively worse, to the
point where "milk was not enough. I would want to drink cream. I
would open a box of cereal in the morning and by afternoon, the
whole box of cereal would be gone." In the months before she joined
Overeaters Anonymous, Rosalee was

> taking steaks out of the freezer and fixing myself full dinners at four
> in the morning. I'd sit and eat them on the floor and cry. It is like I
> wasn't thinking. I would wake up from a terrible night and think:
> food. In the kitchen like a zombie. Start fixing, defrost, and just sit
> there and shovel right in. . . . My whole being was centered around
> food. This was something that had been getting increasingly worse.

Nicole describes her eating problems in three increasingly severe
stages. In stage one, during her childhood, bingeing was neither conscious nor deliberate. She binged on whatever food was available and
felt neither guilt nor remorse. During stage two, which began in college, bingeing became much more deliberate; for the first time, she began to steal food and to buy it in bulk. She attempted many diets and
went on bingeing sprees with her best friend, who taught her to be bulimic. She was bingeing and purging for the same reasons she had
binged in childhood—racist exclusion at school and her mother's
physical and emotional abuse—but it had begun to be debilitating.
Stage three began after college. She binged "no holds barred" and
gained a lot of weight, topping three hundred pounds. In stage three,

I would be eating in order to get to the place I was going to get food to binge with. My skid row period. All of my day revolved around food. Everything—school, work, and people—were secondary to that. . . . It was a whole other stage for me. . . . It wasn't any more emptying out to fill it up again. Purging was an integral part of the binge . . . bingeing and throwing up were the goal. One was not relieving the other. That is when I would say I really had an eating disorder. It was deliberate but it was uncontrollable. The terror and pain and self-hate as well as, I just learned in working with my therapist, a sense of soothing came from the bulimia. . . . The consistency of it [purging] was soothing, but it was also terrifying because I was afraid I would kill myself. I would throw up until I saw blood and then that would be the only thing that would stop me for that moment. I feared a lot that I would choke. The only thing that would stop me is when I would see blood.

By stage three, the control over bingeing and purging she had when she was younger was gone as the physiological addiction to purging began to take hold. At this point, Nicole was in extreme physical danger since she could not stop herself from throwing up. What had begun as a protective response had turned on her, leading her to reach out for help.

The trajectory of most of the women's eating difficulties, however, was not as overtly progressive, which suggests that the framework of eating problems as an addictive disease cannot be applied universally.[12] Many women binged, purged, or dieted during stressful or traumatic times: when the stress diminished, their problems with food subsided too; increased stress would cause their eating problems to flare up again. But—unlike those of the women whose eating problems were progressive and addictive—these eating patterns were no more intense than they had been during previous times in the women's lives.[13]

In general, intermittent eating problems tended to be less physically and psychologically harmful than those described as progressive addictions. Among the women who characterized eating problems as progressive, most had been through several traumas when they were very young children. In addition, they appeared to have fewer means of escaping their pain than those whose eating problems flared up and subsided in response to specific stresses. For example, three women whose eating problems were progressive and addictive were African-American women who endured various types of abuse at home and experienced racist exclusion at school. Facing trauma both privately and publicly, they had nowhere to escape pain.

Those who described not being able to leave their bodies as children were among those whose eating problems became progressively worse, to the point of becoming life-threatening. This suggests that leaving their bodies in the face of trauma may have protected some of the women from long-term consequences in a way not afforded to those who did not or could not escape psychically or physically. Whether the women's eating problems were progressive or intermittent, what began as helpful methods of coping eventually became impediments they decided to change.

The progression of eating problems over time illuminates why a strategy of resistance against a hostile and injurious environment is not necessarily the same as a strategy for liberation. In their research on African-American adolescent girls, Tracy Robinson and Janie Victoria Ward explain that while

> African-American people, particularly women, have become expert developers and appropriators of resistant attitudes, we believe that all these forms of resistance are not always in our best interest.[14]

Some methods of coping may serve women in the short term but may be counterproductive psychically or physically over the long term. The progression of eating problems is a powerful example of how and why eating is not a strategy of liberation.[15] As Ann Kearney-Cooke explains, "mechanisms that allow for psychic survival as an abused child become impediments for effective coping as an adult."[16]

With the right resources and sources of support, the women I talked to began to heal—to develop sane relationships to food and their bodies—and to make the transition from surviving to flourishing, from resistance toward liberation.

6 In the Mourning There Is Light

Dear goddess! Face-up again against the renewal of vows.
Do not let me die a coward, mother. Nor forget how to
sing. Nor forget song is a part of mourning as light is a
part of sun.

Audre Lorde[1]

Silence is like starvation. Don't be fooled. It's nothing
short of that, and felt most sharply when one has had a
full belly most of her life. When we are not physically
starving, we have the luxury to realize psychic and
emotional starvation. It is from this starvation that other
starvations can be recognized.

Cherríe Moraga[2]

Toward the Light

A holistic healing process — involving the mind, body, and spirit —
draws on innovative and creative strategies. The healing methods developed by the women I interviewed reflect tenacity and a willingness
to recreate what was injured or destroyed by trauma. Healing
mirrored — was the reverse of — the trauma, a discovery of aspects of
themselves long lost or hidden from view. Only a few sought medical
or therapeutic help; many of their strategies are not considered in medical and psychological scholarship on eating problems.[3] Their insights
have important implications for future treatment and prevention.

The diversity of backgrounds and the range of eating problems of
the women I talked with makes way for an expansive understanding of
healing. While some of them have just begun to heal, others are far
along in the process. Those in the early stages typically consider healing to be contingent on attaining a certain weight. For those farther
along, the definition of healing became much more expansive as they
examined the meaning of their eating problems, why they developed,
how they progressed, and what function they had served; many have

come to respect how their eating strategies began as methods of survival. For them, healing means being able to enjoy eating, believing
they have the right to eat, and learning to stop eating when they are
full. It has been a dynamic long-term process rooted in racial, sexual,
and religious identity and dependent on access to time, money, and
support.

Years of going around in circles often preceded stumbling on or being directed to a successful approach. Many of the women tried diets
and weight loss clinics, which typically brought a temporary loss of
pounds they eventually regained. Descriptions of failed diets provided
comic relief in our conversations: the hot dog and banana diet, the
grapefruit diet, the all-protein or no-protein diet, the diet that required
drinking virtual swimming pools of water. Poking fun at the weekly
weigh-in process at Weight Watchers, Laura said:

> Everybody would take everything dignified off before getting on the
> scale to get weighed. Bracelets came off. Everything. Change in the
> pockets came out. Socks if they were on the heavy side would come
> off.

Underneath the laughter was deep frustration about how others—
and sometimes they themselves—interpreted their worries about eating superficially, as attempts to "look good" and count calories.
Meanwhile, the underlying traumas were seldom addressed. Losing
weight drew praise, even if they dropped far below a healthy weight at
a pace that jeopardized their physical and mental well-being. Being
"overweight" continued to garner negative attention, but none of the
women was ever approached by family or friends worried about del-
eterious effects of significant weight fluctuations or weight loss. In no
case did a family member or friend ask about anorexia or bulimia.

Everyone missed the signs of eating problems—out of negligence or
sheer ignorance. Some of the women sought medical help for physical
symptoms partially related to eating problems, but their doctors did
not recognize the symptoms or did not know how to ask about the
psychological dimensions of their ailments. Formal diagnosis of eating
problems took years, and, in fact, most of those who were anorexic or
bulimic have yet to be diagnosed by a medical professional. While
there is some benefit in avoiding the stigma of diagnosis and the un-
necessary medical restrictions associated with some treatments, there
were also negative consequences. In particular, when eating problems
became liabilities, the women did not have a term that might have
helped them seek support.

A combination of persistence, stubbornness, and luck led to some
effective approaches. When Rosalee was constantly bingeing—and

depressed—she began to have heart palpitations and thought she was going to have a heart attack. She checked herself into the hospital for tests; she was given sleeping pills and blood pressure medication and released. The palpitations continued, as did the depression. She was hospitalized again, but received contradictory diagnoses because the doctors considered her panic attacks, fluctuating blood pressure, and heart problems to be purely physical symptoms. They continued to treat her eating problem as an issue of self-control and recommended that she diet. Next she sought help from a psychiatrist, who diagnosed dysthymia disorder and prescribed more sleeping pills. When Rosalee looked this diagnosis up and learned that it meant suffering from a sense of hopelessness, she was frustrated by how obvious it was:

> It is easier for them to eventually prescribe a pill for why you can't sleep than to talk about the nightmares waking you up. . . . I began to lose faith in both the medical profession and the psychological field altogether, which left me with my back against the wall.

She felt as if she "was running in the dark and had nothing to go on."

A major life crisis—either positive or negative—motivated several of the women to seek help. Crises have a way of bringing to the fore, and sometimes exaggerating, problems long in existence but difficult to see. Life crises somehow peeled away denial and encouraged the women to be honest about their pain and struggles. Dawn links her father's illness and death from cancer to her decision to seek help. Martha credits the birth of her daughter with her decision to deal with her compulsive eating; she didn't want her daughter to know her as someone "disconnected from the world" and sought to understand how compulsive eating perpetuates disconnection.

A series of failed relationships was another catalyst for seeking help. At the point in Joselyn's life when her bingeing was at its worst—shortly after she dropped out of a graduate program at Harvard in order to start her own business—she was eating compulsively with the man with whom she was living. They would eat "baskets and baskets of food" together: "I mean we ATE . . . I had so much sugar. I remember thinking if I cried it would just come out like saccharine, just tons of sugar." Although *he* didn't gain weight, *she* did—quickly. One evening when they were in bed together, her partner told her he hated her body. Although this was not the first time a man had humiliated her, his insult sent her reeling as she realized how familiar insults had become and how deeply she had internalized them. Finally, Joselyn says, "I started pulling myself together. I got my hair cut, got makeup on, and sought an Overeaters Anonymous meeting."

Deteriorating abilities they considered to be at the core of their per-
sonhood motivated some of the women to take action. For Rosalee,
the courage to stop bingeing came in part from her determination to
recover psychic abilities damaged by sexual abuse. As a child, Rosalee
had remarkable psychic abilities including gifts of clairaudience, clair-
voyance, and precognitive dreams. Sexual abuse diminished Rosalee's
trust in her own instincts and inner abilities and her faith in God. She
says she lost "the ability to be in touch with that essence" because "it
had been twisted and destroyed." As an adult, she began to recover her
clairaudient and clairvoyant talents and served as a medium, which
she defines as being able to "tune into the spirit that goes on beyond
life." Through workshops, seminars, and church conferences, she
taught others how to use their psychic abilities. After a few years of
working as a medium, she began to see violent images that she could
not understand; she could not tell whether they were from her own life
or someone else's. Since she had repressed memories of being sexually
abused, she could not know that these images were flashbacks related
to incest. The flashbacks interfered with her abilities as a medium, hin-
dering her ability to be "the clearest instrument I could be." As the
flashbacks continued, her food habit became increasingly worse. The
flashbacks plus her dissatisfaction with medical professionals encouraged her to seek alternate approaches.

Methods and Dynamics of Healing

Self-help programs were the most common method of healing among
the women. The most common self-help group was Overeaters Anonymous (OA), which is modeled after the twelve-step Alcoholics Anonymous program. In OA meetings, people are encouraged to listen to
others and talk about their own stories of recovery—how food came
to control them, how "abstaining" from addictive eating patterns
changed their lives, what is needed to maintain the change.[4] Overeaters Anonymous taught the women to treat themselves and their ways
of eating more gently by lessening their self-blame. Relief from self-
castigation—which for many began when they were young children—
was a prerequisite to changing their eating patterns. In Overeaters
Anonymous, Antonia heard,

> for the first time in my life, . . . people say that, first of all, it wasn't
> my fault. . . . Secondly, I heard that the reason why I was fat didn't
> really matter. It was a waste of time and energy to try to figure that
> out because you couldn't.

Instead, the focus is on learning how to avoid food that is addictive. The logic behind Overeaters Anonymous is that while it may be useful to, for example, examine emotions and painful incidents in the past, the first task is to "put down the food." The understanding will follow.

This philosophy—that freedom from eating problems is not contingent on articulating their origins—helped the women who desperately wanted to stop dieting and bingeing before they had recovered memories of the trauma underlying their behavior. Antonia was abstinent—which for her meant eating three meals a day, nothing in between, and no sugar—for four years, during which time she lost 80 pounds. Years later she began to piece together how her compulsive eating had begun. For Rosalee, changing her eating habits was essential for recovering complete memories of sexual abuse. She had been plagued by nightmares all her life, but until she stopped bingeing she could not remember her dreams. Compulsive eating had protected her from dream information that would have been difficult to accept, but at the same time it obscured the reasons for the long spells of crying, depression, anxiety, and deep sadness that gnawed at her. Coming to terms with the trauma was dependent on learning not to anesthetize herself with food. Her therapist and the women she met at Overeaters Anonymous gave her the support she needed to understand that she had developed an eating problem as a way to care for herself. As she stopped bingeing, she began to understand that her ability to nurture her psychic abilities depended on both examining her eating patterns and coming to terms with sexual abuse. At this point her heart palpitations and other physical symptoms began to go away, having been the physical manifestations of memories that were beginning to surface.

Overeaters Anonymous proposes an alternative to the popular philosophy that learning to love oneself puts an end to self-destructive eating. Some of the women accepted this perspective at one time in their lives, only to realize that when they continued to binge, they then blamed themselves for not being sufficiently self-loving. Overeaters Anonymous offers a way out of this tangle. The spiritual focus of the program—which emphasizes willingness, motivation, and inspiration rather than self-discipline—concentrates on the present and grounds relief from unwanted food within a larger spiritual frame. Antonia explains:

> The piece of the program that I do really still believe is that I cannot stop it—the allergy or disease—myself. I have to become willing to have it relieved. That has always been my experience whenever I have lost my abstinence and regained it again. It was not about me

deciding I was not going to do any more. It was about me saying, hey, I can't do anything about this. If this is going to stop, something outside of me has got to help. Even if my sense of my higher power is an internalized one, it is still something outside of me, who I am at that moment, that will have to relieve it because I don't think I can.

On the surface, the belief that women cannot, on their own, change their eating patterns suggests an acceptance of powerlessness, a tenet many feminists rightfully have found troubling.[5] Since several of the women were feminists, I was especially interested in how they reckoned with this seeming contradiction. Ironically, accepting their powerlessness to arrest compulsive eating or cycles of dieting alone empowered them by breaking the isolation at the root of their eating problems. Many of the women had a deep-seated and abiding sense of having to "go it alone in the world." Rosalee explains that

> it is not easy for me to let people know how much I hurt. It is a matter of image, pride, and dignity. Having someone know that I hurt that bad, maybe they will know that they can hurt me.

While this is a sensible and sane defensive response to abandonment, it ultimately backfires. Paradoxically, believing they were powerless to stop dieting or bingeing alone empowered the women by grounding their struggles in something larger than themselves—their belief in God, in the group, or in a "higher power" within themselves.[6]

This self-help program enabled the women to speak about haunting secrets they had long since buried. Anonymity is a core aspect of the program. Most of the women had never told anyone about the depth of their eating problems, the sometimes "crazy" things they did with food—eating whole steaks in the middle of the night, cooking and consuming entire boxes of pasta, refusing to eat for days at a time. Their secrets, along with memories of abuse, were burdens that fueled shame and loneliness. Hearing others' stories often encouraged the women to speak themselves. It was in these meetings that many of them first identified themselves as people who had eating problems along with other, even more private, shame-based issues. As philosophers and other theorists have said in various ways, naming something, especially for the first time, inevitably changes it. Rosalee explains:

> OA helped me to understand how to do the deep work. By breaking isolation OA got me to a place in my head where I can stop feeling as if I have to do everything alone.

While half of the women I interviewed considered Overeaters

Anonymous integral to their healing, both those who are still attending and those who have left offered insightful critiques of the program. Overeaters Anonymous helped Vera dramatically—people in OA "deal with the real thing, the pain behind the eating by learning not to use food as a drug to keep emotions down"—but she eventually stopped going to meetings because she was increasingly frustrated by the emphasis on giving up food to which people are emotionally attached.[7] As a Latina, Vera considered attachment to "emotionally charged" food such as rice and beans healthy, not debilitating; she believes it is possible to eat culturally significant foods without overeating. Vera now attends another twelve-step self-help program because it gives her "confidence" and "sanity" and has joined Weight Watchers, which she considers to be, like other diet programs, "semi-crazy" and "semi-sane." This approach helps her eat reasonable portions, a skill she did not learn when she was growing up, while allowing all types of food.

A few of the women criticized what is known as the "gray sheet," a meal plan adopted by some members of Overeaters Anonymous that excludes wheat in any form. While it initially helped break compulsive eating patterns, eventually it seemed unnecessarily restrictive and turned into another form of self-denial. They sought other nutritional plans, often coupling them with the spiritual component of the OA program. Others criticized what they considered to be the judgmental attitudes of some people at OA meetings. Antonia, for example, sought help from Overeaters Anonymous for many years but eventually quit:

> Whereas before I had seen it as home and safety, it started becoming more threatening to me than the general outside world. They would say that eating is not a moral issue . . . but I think that 99 percent of people in OA do somehow believe that eating is a moral issue, even though the rhetoric is that it is not. I don't know anybody who doesn't on some level believe eating is not a moral issue.

Overeaters Anonymous's reputation as a program primarily attended by white people created problems for some of the women of color I interviewed. Joselyn was constantly on guard during meetings, aware that no matter what she said, the white women might think she was speaking for all black women, and this made it hard for her to relax. Rosalee said that it would comfort her if more black women were aware of and attended Overeaters Anonymous, that it

> hurt me and intrigued me at the same time that my becoming aware of OA came from people outside of my race. The support group that I go to is predominantly white. My therapist is a white woman. The people I related to most with this issue are not black people.

Although she has "related well" to one black woman in the program, "having a black face doesn't always mean that people identify with black issues. Even among my own people I have to choose who is for real and who isn't."

Political and historical events beginning with slavery underscore why black women may avoid seeking help for eating problems. As Rosalee says, "admitting to sickness means admitting just one more thing wrong with this black person"—which is made worse when white people are doing the labeling. Breaking through denial on an individual level means confronting the constant assaults on black women's self-esteem—by the media, through sexual violence, and in demeaning depictions of black mothers. Rosalee says the "real issues" underlying eating problems aren't examined when someone as visible and widely respected as Oprah Winfrey—"who has her head together about so much"—diets, but

> dieting is one of those last-ditch efforts to make everything all right
> in your life when that is not the cause of the problems to begin with.
> It is another coping device that keeps us in denial, that keeps us from
> getting to the core issues.

The predominantly white makeup of Overeaters Anonymous makes teasing out the complexities of these issues difficult for black women.

Some women find the decidedly Christian philosophical foundations of Overeaters Anonymous limiting. Turning one's life over to God as one understands "Him"—one of the twelve steps—and the emphasis on confession are fundamentally Christian concepts. Many OA meetings are held in churches—neither inviting nor familiar to many Jewish people.[8] Three Jewish women initiated and participated in a confidential self-help group at their college for students concerned about eating issues. This group helped them break isolation and examine cultural messages about body size and weight without compromising their religious beliefs. One Jewish lesbian was not troubled by OA's Christian focus, but was disturbed by women who seemed to consider their lesbian identities a problem along with their eating difficulties. Discouraged by this, she left the program; when she attended again several years later, she no longer saw evidence of this internalized homophobia.

Despite the program's limitations, its "take what you want and leave the rest" philosophy appeals to a broad spectrum of women. Many of the women I talked with continue to attend and supplement OA activities with others. For example, although several women who sought Overeaters Anonymous consider themselves political activists, none said the professed apolitical stance of the program hindered their attendance.[9] Rather, supplementing the program with their activism enabled them to tolerate this philosophical perspective, although they constantly had to translate into more inclusive terms the references to God as male, Christian-oriented ideas, and heterosexist assumptions. This need for translation is a result of what Patricia Hill Collins calls being an "outsider within," someone who has a unique perspective of an organization's contradictions and limitations. Anyone who is routinely denied access to any kind of power or acceptance—women, men of color, lesbian women and gay men, Jewish people—is likely to be familiar with this perspective in some form.[10] Translating can be both time-consuming and exhausting, particularly in the context of healing.

Counseling helped many of the women change their eating patterns, although none of them sought therapy specifically for this reason.[11] Only as they developed trust in their therapists and worked on psychological problems did therapy help them with their eating problems. This suggests why it is critical for therapists to be knowledgeable about eating problems regardless of their specialties. Some of the women had to change therapists a few times until they found someone with the expertise they needed—a situation that can be especially daunting for women in crisis. The combination of skills they sought included racial and cultural sensitivity and experience in working with lesbians and with people who have been traumatized.[12] For many women, once they found the right person, therapy was intensive, long-term, and profoundly life-affirming. In therapy, they found respect for their feelings and struggles and a means to explore connections between eating and embodiment. As Catherine Steiner-Adair explains, "naming their pain frees women from unconsciously embodying it."[13]

Only two of the eighteen women sought inpatient treatment programs for eating problems. Intensive individual and group therapy during hospitalization helped Dawn understand the effect of sexual abuse, alcoholism, and emotional neglect on her life. The food plan taught her the difference between "grazing" and eating, which helped her "put food in its rightful place" in her life. For Laura, the program itself wasn't as important as the two-month reprieve from daily responsibilities—raising her daughter and working full time—which enabled her to evaluate her life with new eyes:

> Whether it is camping for a month in the woods or going to New York City and spending every dime you have, what matters is that it will enable you to come face to face with yourself, honestly.

Dawn and Laura had insurance that paid for hospitalization—more than twenty-five thousand dollars each. Most of the women couldn't afford such a program without insurance, but many said that getting to the root of their eating problems depended on having time and "permission" to sort through their lives and reassess their methods of coping. Rosalee has been laid off from her job and is currently living on unemployment, which has given her an unexpected but badly needed break from daily life:

> Not working is a blessing in disguise. When an issue comes up, when I wake up in the morning and there is something there, I can take the time to work through it, through my journal, through my writing. Before, when I was working and I'd go to therapy on my lunch hour, I'd come back and my eyes were red. . . . It is just too much of a hassle to deal with work and that too. Now I come home and continue crying if I want. I can face those issues I didn't have time to look at. When you are living in a society that is as rushed as ours and you are trying to deal with issues that need to be slowly uncovered then gently solved, it is almost impossible to deal with that kind of stuff and keep up a job, a family, etc.

In order to heal, Rosalee, like many women, needed a chance to be herself without having to "change her face" for others, to care for other people, or to worry about others' responses to her emotions. Opal Palmer Adisa explains in her essay on stress and black women:

"Stress!"

"Girl, ain't that the truth."

"Needing to have a change of face to put on depending on the occasion wears on my body."

"Always having to think six steps ahead, then some, is what gets to me."

"What I need is a rocking chair . . . "

"And the sun light to rock under . . . "[14]

The long process of uncovering trauma is one reason we need afford-able health insurance that covers treatment of post-traumatic stress disorder; sexual, physical, and emotional abuse; traumatic conse-quences of hate crimes; and eating problems and addiction to other substances: healing requires time to "rock in the sunlight." Despite the contemporary negative connotations of the word *disease*, its Latin roots suggest that healing depends on having unencumbered time. In Latin, *disease* means no elbows, no elbow room. Ease is a form of pleasure, disease a loss of pleasure.[15] Those who have been hurt need room to spread out, need to have time for pleasure, to be free to imag-ine themselves in new ways.

The Right to Feel

The role of trauma in the development of eating problems illustrates why healing depends on a woman's learning that she has a right to feel. For some of the women I interviewed this meant learning they *had* feelings, which was a prerequisite to understanding how feelings affected their actions, including eating patterns. Many had long since stopped feeling on a conscious level. Barraged by incidents far too outrageous and cruel to make sense of at the time they occurred, they turned off their feelings. Frequently, these incidents had flooded them with such unfamiliar and confusing feelings that blocking feelings or shutting down entirely was a protection against madness.[16] As Joselyn explains, "I didn't have any feeling about how I felt when I ate. I didn't know that there were feelings there, because for years they were stripped away from me." This made the process of opening up to new feelings and acknowledging old ones extremely scary. Identifying how painful emotions fueled their eating problems often began when the women started to notice what they were feeling when they most wanted to binge or to deny themselves food. Then they tried to understand that emotion rather than eat. Many of them had gotten into the habit of eating compulsively even before they had a chance to feel emotions and, as a consequence, did not know what triggered their desire to eat. For many of them, initial attempts to identify feelings were disorienting and threatening. They had trouble differentiating between feelings — between sadness and anger, for example — or their feelings seemed to be free-floating. Healing required them to tether these emotions, to trace the feelings back to their sources. This meant learning to identify whether the feelings were related to a recent incident or if an emotion from the past was triggered by a recent event.[17] Carolyn, for example, often came home after work and binged, although she always promised herself she would not. After she stopped eating compulsively, she began to understand the factors that triggered a binge: when her boss had treated her in a racist and sexist way, she binged, never acknowledging her anger and frustration to herself or her boss. When she ate, her anxiety diminished as the food calmed her. Over time, however, she began to realize that by eating she was also punishing herself. Bingeing made her feel lethargic and uncomfortable, and she was no closer to knowing what feelings preceded the binge. By not anesthetizing herself with food, she began to acknowledge her anger and frustration, which made her better able to deal with racist incidents. For Carolyn and many other women, the essence of healing was not denying themselves food but rather making distinctions between physical hunger and the hunger that signals uncomfortable emotions and learning to respond to these two types of hunger in different ways.

One of the hardest tasks for many of the women has been to treat uncomfortable feelings—including their negative feelings about their bodies—as signposts for further recovery. Often these feelings came in waves that coincide with memories of abuse. Although Antonia had not eaten compulsively for years, around the time she began to get "emotional memories of the incest," she began to binge again. While she acknowledged bingeing as a form of nurturing, it pained her that she was coping that way again. She has been especially distraught by her weight gain but has had a hard time admitting this openly. She has been a feminist for all of her adult years, an antiracist activist who has worked in a shelter for battered women—experiences that she believes have facilitated her ability to resist cultural expectations about thinness. Yet according to her current understanding of healing, she must admit to herself that her weight (about two hundred pounds) is completely unacceptable to her. Ironically, she considers this declaration an act of self-love, because she is no longer pretending to like what she so much wants to change. Given Antonia's history, her present deep attachment to the idea of a thinner body makes perfect sense. Since she has only recently uncovered the memories of the incest she endured, she has just begun to understand how and why it caused her to dissociate from her body. Fat was the alien, the physical manifestation of her grandfather's abuse. Understanding this helps explain why being fat has made her feel such disdain about herself of late—for a long time, fat was the marker of sexual violation and invasion of her bodily integrity—and why no amount of consciousness of the misogyny underlying the culture of thinness could make her ease up on herself about gaining weight. Gaining weight again felt like being abused again. Further healing rests in part on redirecting her anger away from her body and toward those who hurt her. While she may or may not lose weight in the process, being able to live comfortably in her body depends on being free of the feeling that her body will forever carry the physical sign of abuse.

Fighting Back and Other Affirmations

Some of the women's attempts to re-create what was injured or stolen from them by trauma took the form of affirming their racial and sexual identities. Not surprisingly, those who consider such an affirmation most central to their healing are those whose racial and sexual identities had been most under attack. Two of the African-American women were raised in families that supported and celebrated their black identity, while three were raised by parents or other relatives whose internalized racism hindered their racial development. For these three women, developing positive racial identities has been integral to establishing new eating patterns. A trip to Egypt was a crucial beginning in Rosalee's process of claiming a positive sense of herself as a black woman. She wanted to see the roots of black culture before slavery; her journey paralleled her need to recover the psychic abilities she had before being sexually abused. In Egypt, she was able to "see a sea of brown faces and be considered beautiful." Because Christianity is the backbone of her identity, going to mosques where paintings of a black Jesus predominated was "one of the most empowering experiences I have ever had." After returning from Egypt, she designed a shrine and altar in her living room that houses three sculptures of a brown-skinned Jesus, a statue of an Egyptian woman in black and gold, and candles and stones set in formations she saw in Egypt. Her shrine symbolizes her vision of Christianity and a religious tradition that embraces her black identity. In addition to Overeaters Anonymous, Rosalee joined a black women's self-help group called Phenomenal Woman:[18]

> I have been searching high and low to find a support group that would consist of my sisters, meaning black women. I feel a kind of kinship with all races, and I can really say that from a humanitarian point of view. In OA and Al-Anon meetings I have seen how much we suffer from the same things, which has just done so much to open my heart. But by the same token, there are issues that I need to deal with that are exclusively black that I want to deal with with black women. I see it as a necessary separation until we get a hold on who we are.

For Antonia, healing has meant finding a community where she feels valued as an Italian-American lesbian and a woman of stature and size. She lives and works with African-American, Latina, and white women, and she feels more acceptance for being assertive than she did growing up in an overwhelmingly WASP town. Learning about her own racial identity and about racism in the United States has been key to her self-acceptance, including her relationship to her body and to food.[19]

The affirmation of racial identity often coincided with reclaiming sexuality. At the root of many of the women's eating problems were sexual abuse, heterosexism, racist stereotypes about black and Latina women, and the objectification of women's bodies — all of which jeopardize a woman's sense of herself as a sexually whole human being. Coming to terms with the past required uncovering and sorting through gendered and racist humiliations aimed at designating their bodies, attitudes, and movements inappropriate or intolerable. Often, this process required identifying how they had been violated sexually as children and the effect on their sexual lives as adults. Joselyn, for example, realized that she typically "loses" herself in sexual relationships and has based her opinion of herself and her body on men's evaluations. When she is sexually involved, "there are no boundaries. And it is not like I absorb someone else's; it is like I am absorbed into that other person." Finding her own perspectives, including her own opinion about her body, depended on examining how a combination of sexual abuse and racism had whittled away at her psychological and physical boundaries.

For many of the women, sexual healing began with determining when and how they had internalized the idea that they had no right to be sexual. For fat women, this includes claiming the right to sexual pleasure despite the barrage of images that desexualize them. For some of the women, losing weight softened their own harsh judgments about their bodies, which gave them confidence to express themselves sexually. Many linked the end of bingeing and becoming sexually involved for the first time. This connection made some wonder if what they had thought was self-imposed celibacy was actually a consequence of living in a society that is phobic about fat. But even those who maintained long-term weight loss eventually realized that their new body shapes did not guarantee continued self-acceptance—that long-term affirmation of sexuality has less to do with weight and more to do with positive and supportive relationships, healing from trauma, and other forms of empowerment.

Affirming sexuality often hinged on reevaluating scenes indelibly carved in their memories that had made them uncomfortable about sexuality. One woman remembers having always cringed when men told her they would date her if she lost weight; it did not occur to her until adulthood that regardless of her weight, she might not have wanted to date them. For many of these women, reestablishing a sense of themselves as sexual beings meant facing down the emotional ghosts that haunted them because of repressed or painful memories of sexual abuse. Some had trained themselves to turn off their feelings during abuse—an act of basic survival—but this made it hard for them to let go and enjoy sexual pleasure, even when sex was desired and not abusive.[20] Some were left with deep-seated feelings that their bodies had betrayed them during abuse. Some had become physically aroused during the abuse, which engendered much shame and self-blame; such a bodily response can make a girl think she somehow asked for or wanted the abuse. Affirming a positive sexual identity demands believing that physical arousal is not the same as consent and that no one deserves or should ever have to endure sexual violation.

Sexual healing in many cases required tracing debilitating messages back to their sources and getting angry about the destruction they had caused. Carolyn recently realized that being sexual and being violent have been one in her mind for as long as she can remember. Years of listening to her father beat her mother in their bedroom taught her that sexual behavior and violence were inevitably intertwined. As she stopped bingeing, she recovered these memories, a step that has helped her retrieve sexual feelings and memories that have been too frightening to acknowledge. Distinguishing between previously conflated emotions was a step toward developing a full range of feelings. In the process, she began to acknowledge shame she had long felt about how she took her anger out on herself and others when she was growing up. Developing an affectionate understanding of all of their responses to abuse—including their use of food—was central to the survivors' ability to claim their sexual feelings in the present.

Among the lesbians, coming out played a pivotal role in claiming a positive sexual identity. They spoke of it as a release of life-affirming energy, as an exhilarating, frightening process that frequently coincided with a dramatic change in their eating patterns and weight loss. For Martha, meeting lesbians who felt comfortable with their sexual identities and falling in love with a woman coincided with losing fifty pounds. This was the first time she remembers having feelings and knowing she actually exists. Weight loss signaled a transition from reaching for food for comfort to turning to people instead. Similarly, Ruthie made a direct connection between claiming her lesbian identity and worrying less about her body size, which helped her stop dieting. In Nicole's relationships with women, she began to open up parts of herself that had been smothered when she was a child. Because of her mother's emotional and physical abuse, Nicole did not have a friend until she left home for college. Her first close friendship was with a woman with whom she binged, which broke Nicole's silence about her eating problems. During her early adulthood, a woman unexpectedly gave her a big kiss, and she felt sexually alive for the first time in her life. Nicole's friendships with other black lesbians and other feminists of color have been at the heart of her recovery, partly because they gave her the courage and confidence she needed to face childhood trauma. This community, along with Overeaters Anonymous and therapy, eventually led her to stop bingeing and purging.

Although the lesbians see coming out as a significant and positive turning point in their relationships to food, being part of a lesbian community has not necessarily made them more accepting of their bodies in the long run. Some of the lesbians say that when they first came out, they expected other lesbians to have less rigid and more accepting ideas about beauty than they experienced among heterosexuals; unfortunately, many found the same exacting standards among lesbians. While lesbian feminist writing and activism opposing dominant standards of beauty can be a source of power for women recovering from eating problems, lesbians may be no less cruel to each other about weight and size than heterosexuals are. Health care professionals who work with lesbians with eating problems must both respect lesbian culture and refuse to romanticize it. Although lesbian feminist theorists have been at the forefront in developing a political analysis of fat oppression, this work is not done.[21]

Coming out as a lesbian is often much more like walking through a complicated maze than like emerging out of a single closet, and the women's use of food to cope with this process is equally complex. Several of them attribute their ability to stop starving or bingeing to the initial excitement of coming out. The transformation gave them energy and often brought them into contact with supportive people, which countered the isolation and alienation of many of their childhoods. But claiming a lesbian identity also means facing homophobia among family members and old friends, which encourages a retreat into old methods of coping. When Julie was first coming out, she felt joyful and experienced a reprieve from extreme dieting, but homophobic reactions made her feel as if others no longer saw her, and she "felt empty inside." Bingeing made her feel "filled up again"; she had trouble knowing that her feelings exist even if others don't acknowledge or approve of her or her choices.

Political activism can link healing to larger historical and political struggles both as an affirmation and as a method of empowerment. African-American women got involved with other African-Americans and in multiracial alliances. Most of the Latinas are activists at college, in their workplaces, or in their neighborhoods. Many of the lesbians — black, Latina, and white — coupled coming out with political activism.

Working at a shelter for battered women or answering a rape crisis hot line helps survivors of sexual and emotional abuse direct their anger away from themselves and toward those who hurt them, while it helps them gain respect for how they resisted abuse. Antonia says:

> Before I came to grips with having been raped, I was doing rape education and training in a feminist organization. One day I was attending a conference and I realized I had been raped. One of the most beautiful things that came out of the feminist movement is the assumption that when you are in a rape situation, absolutely anything

you do to get out of it alive is a valid strategy. Anything. I don't care how disgusting it might be. If you did it and you came out alive, great. I think there is an analogy to coping with eating.

Working in a shelter for battered women provided education about the pervasiveness of violence against women, which the women then applied to their own lives.

Education and community support are other links to larger contexts. After Yolanda returned to college, she stopped gaining weight and began to wear contact lenses and makeup again—all signs of breaking the isolation that had fueled her bingeing. She has also spoken publicly about mothers on welfare, making a bridge between her personal experiences and those of poor women throughout the country. Going to college put Julianna in touch with other Latina students, gave her access to classes that helped her understand alcoholism and its effect on families, and helped her create an identity independent of her role as a daughter in her family.

Dynamic, Evolving Process

Healing is a multidimensional process that twists and turns, and the women often reevaluated and altered their philosophies and approaches. For many of them, a first step was deciding against the severe diets that had led to weight fluctuation. Laura's first approach to her compulsive eating was initiated by her mother, who enforced a strict diet that did nothing to stop her bingeing and caused her enormous frustration:

> I ballooned in high school. Through Weight Watchers I went up and down, up and down. Between 175 and 179 and then between 150 and 179. That is where I bounced like a tennis ball. [In college] I said fuck it. Then I got into some fat serenity, which is also really bad for me. Saying, oh God, I don't care. When I really cared very much. It really hurt me very much. I ended up sleeping with the whole Buffalo police force trying to prove to myself that I didn't care. Four abortions later I decided, oh no, this is not good. I am obviously not really loving myself very much.

In Overeaters Anonymous she stopped eating compulsively and quickly lost sixty pounds. But, after six months of following what she later considered an excessively rigid food plan, she began to binge again. This scared her into seeking out a long-term inpatient treatment program. After a few years in recovery, how much she weighs is for the first time less relevant than eating in a way she considers sane. At 245 pounds, she considers herself healthier than she has ever been. Her fo-

cus is now on eating well and carefully, rather than on how much she
weighs.

Many of the women characterized their healing processes as two
steps forward and one step back. Often they took daring steps toward
acknowledging trauma and learning new methods of coping with pain
yet returned to old coping methods when loneliness, fear, or painful
memories became overwhelming or when crises intervened.[22] Ruthie
told me that

> when you get to a new point in healing, going back is familiar. Even
> when you know it is bad, it is familiar. That is a really lonely place in
> your growth. You get to a place in healing, in spiritual growth, where
> you recognize these patterns. . . . You don't want to go back but that
> is what is familiar. Back to bad behaviors whether it be with eating,
> friendships, or your relationship to your parents.

For many of the women, healing was a slow process because of the
many layers of trauma they needed to sort through. Rosalee is a vivid
case in point. Changing her eating patterns has been intertwined with
seeking help for having grown up with an alcoholic father, incest, battery by her former husband, and her own possible alcoholism. As she
begins this formidable task, she has learned that she has to pace herself. The first time she spoke at an Al-Anon meeting about growing up
with an alcoholic father, she began to cry so hard that she couldn't
stop. She was so embarrassed that she quit abruptly, telling herself she
was actually fine. Later she went back, and with help from Al-Anon,
therapy, and Overeaters Anonymous, began to retrieve memories she
had repressed since childhood—of a cousin who was smothered to
death by parents who were "disciplining" him, of her feelings about
her daughter, who had "not been conceived in love," of sexual abuse.
Stopping bingeing gave her a window to many buried memories, yet
this clarity left her terrified; after a month she began to binge again,
although not as much as before:

> During times like this, I feel like I am just skating on thin ice. Like I
> am about to go under. I start grasping. I was talking to my pastors. I
> was angry with God. I am going to church. I am being as good a
> person as I know how to be and still my life is falling apart and I feel
> like shit. Physically I am falling apart. . . . I have been through so
> much stuff and there is so much stuff down there it scares the hell
> out of me. It really does. I am at the point now where I have days
> when I honestly don't know if I can continue. I get emotional about
> this because of all the things I have tried to salvage, out of what I
> consider a kind of crummy life. It is much worse than I ever thought.
> It is much worse than I thought I could have ever dealt with. I

needed to bury it because I simply wouldn't have been able to function.

Dawn's substitution of one drug for another contributed to a bumpy healing process. She found some relief from bingeing when she began to attend OA meetings, but when she came out as a lesbian she tabled her involvement in the program. Then her partner became abusive and attempted to kill her, which petrified her and brought her back to meetings again—this time to both Alcoholics Anonymous and Overeaters Anonymous. She became involved with another woman who was an addict and they began to freebase cocaine for hours and sometimes days at a time. After using all of her savings, she realized that while the company she was keeping certainly was encouraging her addiction, it was not the cause. When she stopped bingeing and purging she lost weight, which gave her confidence to get sexually involved. As the infatuation wore off, however, she would begin to use whatever drug was closest at hand. With each step she understood more fully the signs of denial and distraction that had stood in her way.

Martha linked coming out as a lesbian with her initial willingness to stop bingeing. Her emerging lesbian identity gave her energy she had never felt as someone who had spent her life watching television for twelve hours a day. She began to exercise, visit people, and go to parties for the first time in her life. In a summer's time she lost sixty pounds. She also began to smoke marijuana, which she now believes became a compulsion the way that bingeing had. Ironically, because she was getting high with people when she smoked rather than bingeing by herself, smoking pot was a step toward rather than away from healing; she was beginning to break the isolation at the root of her disconnection. By her late twenties she realized she was addicted to pot and had been told by her therapist that she could not come to therapy stoned. Martha sought a twelve-step drug treatment program and stopped smoking pot, then began to binge again and gained fifty pounds. In retrospect, she doesn't think she ever fully confronted her eating problems during the years her bingeing subsided since she had substituted one drug for another. By the time she stopped smoking pot and realized she needed help for her compulsive eating, more resources were available to her than when she was younger. She had been introduced to the philosophy of twelve-step programs, which made attending Overeaters Anonymous familiar. She had been in therapy for a few years and knew that her weight gain wasn't simply a matter of needing more self-control. Her years of involvement in the lesbian community had significantly lessened the internalized homophobia that had been at the root of the shame and isolation she felt as a child. After pregnancy and the birth of her daughter, Martha had trouble losing the 95 pounds she had gained during the pregnancy. All of these factors led her to continue therapy and seek Overeaters Anonymous.

An Expansive Project

Ultimately, the women I interviewed used a combination of healing strategies, either because one was not sufficient in itself or because an approach that brought relief and support at one point in a woman's life failed to do so later. Their many approaches speak to the multilayered dimensions of eating problems. On the surface they involve issues of nutrition and eating patterns; on a deeper level, freeing oneself of them requires concerted long-term attention to psychological health; sexual, racial and religious affirmations; and access to community resources and support.

The link between healing and the decline of bingeing and dieting is complicated by the cyclical and evolving definition of healing. A few women who initially considered bingeing a problem eventually softened their assessments. Although all of the women identified their bingeing, purging, and compulsive eating as painful liabilities, they were careful to note that these actions are far superior to many other ways of responding to pain and injustice.

Vera had been eating compulsively less often for several years when a very close friend died, leaving Vera and her lesbian partner with the friend's two small children. The women became deeply attached to the children and embraced parenthood wholeheartedly, then lost the children to relatives who objected to lesbian parents. Actively alcoholic and aggressively homophobic, these people neglected the children and refused Vera and her partner further contact with them. Vera's grief about this enormous loss and her powerlessness to protect the children brought on despair and depression. She continued to attend Overeaters Anonymous as she had for several years, but for the first time she fell fast asleep during the meetings—the closest she had ever come to leaving her body. She realized that the emotional trauma was "more than I could handle" and became increasingly skeptical of the philosophy that people should avoid bingeing "no matter what." She began to gain weight quickly and soon tried, to no avail, tactics—Slim Fast and Dexatrim—she had given up years before. She knew from experience the dangers of cycles of weight loss and gain that diets can cause and decided against further quick fixes. She also reassessed the notion of bingeing as an addiction, ultimately discarding that philosophy as too harsh and too rigid. She now considers bingeing a compulsion rather than an addiction, and while she intends not to use food to "keep emotions down" she believes her new outlook is less critical, more flexible, and ultimately more loving.

Vera's experience raises the question of whether there is something inherently wrong with using food as a comfort when something terrible occurs. If it soothes someone in a time of extraordinary grief — why not? For some of the women, a sign of recovery was coming to see eating as a reasonable way to cope with adversity given other "choices." These questions bring the discussion full circle, since answering them rests on social and political analysis. The "just say no to food and yes to life" approach to eating problems, like the "just say no to drugs" ideas of the Reagan-Bush years, reduces complex issues of social justice and access to resources to psychological issues of self-control and will power. As long as the violence and social injustices that women link to the origins and perpetuation of their eating problems exist, women may continue to binge, purge, and starve themselves.

The link between eating problems and the traumas these eighteen women described to me indicates that prevention of eating problems depends on changing the social conditions that support violence and injustice. Making it possible for women to have healthy relationships with their bodies and their food is a comprehensive task: we need to ensure that children grow up free of racism and sexual abuse, that parents have adequate resources to raise their children, and that young lesbians have a chance to see their reflection in their teachers and community leaders. We must confront the myth of a monolingual society and support multilingual education; change a welfare system in which a household that is eligible for the maximum amount of assistance receives an average of forty cents worth of food stamps per meal;[23] dismantle the alliance of the medical, insurance, reducing, and advertising industries that capitalizes on reducing women's bodies to childlike sizes; refuse to blame women who are anorexic or bulimic; and dispel the notion that large women automatically eat too much. Women must learn to feed themselves along with — not after — others. Ultimately, the prevention of eating problems depends on economic, cultural, racial, political, and sexual justice.

Women with eating problems need access to healing strategies that support the development of positive racial and sexual identity, since these are keys to self-esteem and empowerment. Those who seek therapy deserve multiracial and multicultural counseling in public and private agencies that employ women of color and lesbians at all levels. Health professionals must be willing to, in the words of Maria Root, "take the initiative to be culturally literate with a diversity of cultural groups."[24] Programs for women with eating problems need to include at all levels—staff, administration, and board—people who know, from experience, about eating problems.

Effectively combating eating problems across the lines of class, race, religion, and ethnicity hinges on understanding that there are many possible approaches: going to Egypt, getting financial aid to attend college, working for a rape crisis hot line, becoming an athlete, seeking counseling, becoming an activist, joining a self-help group. Long-term healing is often born of counseling coupled with involvement in community, political, educational, and religious organizations. A therapist's ability to support a multifaceted approach to healing often depends on willingness to build multiracial, multicultural bridges, both personally and professionally. Such a commitment may determine whether women of color and working-class women seek and benefit from treatment—and can change the epidemiological portrait that hinders a comprehensive understanding of the causes of eating problems and the methods of healing from them.

Biographical Sketches

Note: All of the names are pseudonyms. In order to protect the women's anonymity, some details have been changed or intentionally left vague.

Antonia is a thirty-five-year-old white Italian-American lesbian who grew up in West Virginia in a working-class Catholic family with her mother, father, two sisters, and several of her extended family. She began to eat compulsively when she was four years old; she now believes this was a response to incest. Her bingeing as a child was exacerbated by being a cultural outsider (an Italian-American growing up in a WASP town) and the humiliation she endured as a chunky child. Her adult weight has fluctuated between 133 and 230 pounds. Overeaters Anonymous, Al-Anon, and therapy have helped her, along with working as an antiracism activist and living in a multiracial community. She has a bachelor of arts degree, has completed some doctoral work, and is currently directing a community-based multicultural educational agency.

Carolyn is a thirty-one-year-old African-American married heterosexual woman. The youngest of four children, she was raised in a middle-class Protestant family in New York City. She links the origins of her compulsive eating, which began when she was six years old, to witnessing her father's battery of her mother and the children. Her adult weight has fluctuated between 140 and 200 pounds. Overeaters Anonymous, books on meditation, and feminist scholarship on women's bodies and eating have helped her "explore her feelings" instead of "stuffing the food in." She has a college degree, is a talented seamstress, loves music, works full time as an administrator, and has recently become pregnant.

Dawn is a twenty-nine-year-old white lesbian woman who grew up in an upper middle class Roman Catholic family with her mother, father, and four siblings in a Boston suburb. Her problems with eating, including bulimia and anorexia, began when she was eight and continued through adulthood; her weight has fluctuated between 117 and 150 pounds. She links her food addiction to an extreme emphasis on food restriction and weight control in her family, to molestation, and to emotional neglect. She has also been addicted to cocaine, Valium, speed, and alcohol. Twelve-step programs and a two-month inpatient treatment program have been integral to her healing; she has been "in recovery" for the past fifteen months. She works full time in a travel agency.

Elsa is a forty-six-year-old heterosexual woman who grew up in an upper-class family in Buenos Aires, Argentina. Number six of seven children, she was raised primarily by German governesses. She began to use food as "an emotional filler" when she was eleven and has struggled with anorexia, dieting, and compulsive eating ever since; her weight has fluctuated between 120 and 215-plus pounds. She was put on a number of severe diets and prescribed amphetamines for weight loss during adolescence. She attributes her eating troubles and "hating my body" to a variety of factors in her childhood: emotional abuse by her father, neglect by her mother, exceptionally rigid care, sexual abuse, and patriarchal expectations that she marry, have children, and not have a career. As she says, "I sort of graduated from being a daughter to being a wife with very little control over my life." Several years ago she moved, with her husband, two adult daughters, and a teenage son to a suburb of Boston and has recently separated from her husband after twenty-seven years of marriage. Although Elsa is still caught up in cycles of dieting and bingeing, she has "discovered newfound strength" by moving away from her family and coming to the United States, separating from her husband, and getting a good job. After having to wait several years for immigration papers that allow her to work, she is now working full time, and loving it, as a translator for refugees from El Salvador. Being fat has felt to Elsa as if the "real me was fifteen layers into myself, like an onion." She believes that healing is dependent on getting thin and "not being hungry any more."

Gilda is a twenty-one-year-old Sephardic Jewish lesbian woman who lived with her mother, father, siblings, and extended family in North Africa and France before the family settled in New York City. French was her first language. Her nuclear family's financial stability fluctuated considerably; eventually they settled into the upper middle class. She links the beginnings of her compulsive eating, extensive dieting, and weight fluctuation (155 to 250 pounds) in part to being raped when she was eleven years old, an experience she immediately "forgot." When she remembered the rape when she was 16, she attempted suicide and gained 110 pounds. She also ties her bingeing and dieting to the clashing cultural expectations that resulted from her family's intercontinental moves. And she binged to cope with an abusive relationship (she was 13 to 17 years old) during which she was kidnapped and was physically abused so badly that she had to be hospitalized. She sees herself as just beginning to heal; she has only recently understood the connection between sexual abuse and bingeing and is still using food in ways she considers harmful. She recently completed a three-month liquid protein diet that caused a stomach ulcer and made her unable to eat solid food without purging. The experiences that have most helped her accept her body and her eating patterns have been coming out as a lesbian, which she describes as "the most liberating thing I have ever done for myself," and working at a shelter for battered women and for a rape crisis hot line. She recently graduated from college and continues to work at a shelter in a Boston suburb.

Jackie is a twenty-eight-year-old white lesbian woman who was raised in a Protestant family in northern California. Her mother divorced when Jackie was five and remarried shortly thereafter. She has a biological brother and sister and several siblings from her mother's second marriage. Her mother's economic status fluctuated with the divorce; eventually they became an upper middle class family. She first wondered if she was a lesbian when she was young, and she came out during high school. She was bulimic between the ages of fifteen and eighteen; bingeing and dieting have caused her weight to fluctuate between 140 and 190 pounds. She links her eating problems to homophobia, sexism, and anger about the divorce. She attributes her healing to evolving a positive sexual identity as a lesbian, moving away from her family, understanding "the politics of gender," and being an athlete. Although she would still like to feel more comfortable with her weight and her body, she "no longer feel[s] victimized by an eating problem," eats without feeling guilty, and no longer binges. She has a bachelor of arts degree, is currently a reporter at a gay and lesbian community newspaper, plays on a women's softball team, and lives with her lover in Boston.

Joselyn is a thirty-five-year-old African-American heterosexual woman who lived with her mother, father, brother, sister, and grandmother in Queens, New York. Her family, "aspiring to be middle class," moved into the upper middle class while she was growing up. She was raised Catholic and attended parochial schools. She links her compulsive eating, extensive dieting, and laxative use to mixed messages about food and pressure to diet from her family, her father's and grandmother's emotional and physical abuse, which was laced with racism and classism, and sexual abuse. Her adult weight has fluctuated from 130 to 210 pounds. Overeaters Anonymous (for four years) and therapy (for five years), along with nurturing her artistic and intellectual talents have given her insight into her body and her appetite. She has a bachelor of arts degree from Harvard, writes poetry, collects antiques, and currently works in a fancy women's clothing store. She has recently sought career counseling, hoping to find work that draws on her writing abilities.

Julianna is a twenty-four-year-old heterosexual woman raised in a Spanish-speaking middle-class Catholic family by her grandmother and other members of her extended family in the Dominican Republic. When she was sixteen she and her younger brother moved to Boston to join her mother, father, and another brother, who had fled the political repression of the Dominican Republic when Julianna was very young. She attributes her bingeing, bulimia, anorexia, and weight fluctuation (109 to 125 pounds) to stresses of acculturation, her father's alcoholism, and cultural expectations placed on daughters in Dominican families. Getting information about alcoholism, going to college, making friends, and gaining some autonomy from her family helped her heal from her eating problems. She is currently finishing her bachelor of arts degree at the University of Massachusetts at Boston. After graduating she would like to "use what I learned in school, get a good job, use my education, defend my rights, and stand up for myself."

Julie is a twenty-three-year-old white lesbian woman who was adopted with her biological sister into an upper-class Jewish family when she was a newborn and grew up in Rochester, New York. Her eating problems have included anorexia, bulimia, bingeing, and dieting; her weight has fluctuated between 105 and 130 pounds. She links her eating problems to growing up in a family that was obsessed with dieting and weight gain, an emotionally intrusive father, and a sexually and emotionally abusive boyfriend. Attending workshops on women's eating problems, becoming a feminist, coming out as a lesbian, and identifying the abuse she endured have been turning points for her; what used to be a "disorder" are now "eating issues." She recently graduated from a university in Boston and works in a group home for mentally challenged adults.

Laura is a thirty-four-year-old lesbian woman of Puerto Rican, white, and Mexican heritage who lived with her mother, father, and two younger sisters in an English-speaking middle-class Episcopalian family. Her family moved around a lot until she was twelve, leaving her feeling rootless and insecure. She had eating problems—dieting and compulsive eating—as far back as she can remember. Her weight has fluctuated between 150 and 300-plus pounds. She links her eating problems to genetic disposition for food addiction and a family emphasis on thinness and dieting. She describes herself as a "recovering compulsive overeater and alcoholic" whose healing has included a two-month inpatient treatment program and a strict food program associated with a twelve-step program. She considers herself healthier than she has ever been, and is "in a really good time in my life." She has stopped smoking, exercises regularly, and no longer binges or diets. She is the mother of an eight-year-old girl and is in a long-term relationship after coming out as a lesbian two years ago. She works full time in addition to raising her daughter.

Martha is a thirty-seven-year-old white Jewish lesbian who grew up in a working-class family with her mother, father, and three older sisters in Springfield, Massachusetts. She has been eating compulsively on and off since she was eleven years old, and her weight has fluctuated from 140 to 275-plus pounds. She links her eating problems to being "disconnected from the world" as a result of emotional abuse by family members, being put on diets and prescribed powerful diet pills, and trauma caused by heterosexism. She was an alcoholic through her early adult years and has been sober for over a decade. Although she thinks she is "far from healed," she has made progress that she attributes to coming out as a lesbian, getting counseling that helped her feel loved and nurtured her self-esteem, participating in Overeaters Anonymous, learning yoga and getting massages, being a parent, and exercising. She owns a successful business and is raising her daughter with her partner of eight years.

Nicole is a forty-one-year-old lesbian woman of African-American, Cherokee, and white heritage who lived with her mother and father in a middle-class family in Boston, where she attended a number of predominantly white schools and Episcopalian churches. She links her bingeing, which began when she was very young, to racial isolation at school, physical and emotional abuse by her mother stemming from her mother's internalized racism, and discrimination against fat children. Her bulimia and compulsive eating in college (her weight fluctuated between 130 and 310-plus pounds) was also a response to racial isolation and continued familial abuse. Her eating problems became progressively worse, to the point of being life-threatening. Extensive long-term therapy, Overeaters Anonymous, and an inpatient treatment program—which she sought in her thirties because of suicidal feelings—have helped her begin to "find the real self that was buried by the abuse." This has enabled her to stop being bulimic and has lessened her bingeing. Coming out as a lesbian and developing community and friendship ties with other feminists of color helped her claim her sexual and racial identity. She is currently working in the Boston public schools, lives with her long-term lover, and works as a multicultural educator and trainer.

Rosalee is a thirty-six-year-old African-American heterosexual divorced woman who moved around often when she was young (her father was in the army) but primarily grew up in a poor/working-class family in rural Arkansas with her father, mother, three brothers, and two sisters. She links the origins of her compulsive eating, which began when she was four years old, to sexual abuse exacerbated by racism, poverty, and her father's abuse of her mother and the children. In adulthood her weight has fluctuated between 155 and 250 pounds. Her compulsive eating became progressively worse during adulthood, and she sought medical and psychiatric treatment, to no avail. She became extremely distraught, in part because flashbacks of abuse she had not yet identified were interfering with her psychic abilities and her work as a medium. Eventually she found a neo-Reichean therapist who, in combination with Overeaters Anonymous and Al-Anon, enabled her to uncover connections between bingeing and childhood abuse. A trip to Egypt and joining a support group for black women were affirmations of her racial identity. Although she has begun to seek ways of soothing herself other than bingeing, she says healing is like "getting across rough rapids" that will take much time and concerted effort. She has been an administrator for a continuing education program for many years; her employer granted her a paid medical leave that gave her concentrated time to "find the part of me that had been destroyed." Her daughter lives with Rosalee's mother, but she sees her regularly. Rosalee is currently single, and happily so, and eventually hopes to go back to work, although the demands of her previous job may encourage her to seek other employment.

Ruthie is a thirty-four-year-old Puerto Rican lesbian woman who grew up as one of eight daughters in a bilingual (Spanish and English) lower/middle-class Catholic family in New York City. She was bulimic when she was fourteen, fifteen, and sixteen and has struggled with dieting and compulsive eating on and off since that time; her weight has fluctuated between 109 and 150 pounds. She links her eating problems to incest and other sexual abuse and harassment coupled with severe emotional and physical abuse by her mother. She came out as a lesbian during high school, and she attributes developing a more affectionate understanding of her appetite and her body to this affirmation, to therapy, and to feminist activism. The mother of a teenage son, she is currently finishing a bachelor's degree at a university in Massachusetts where she is a campus activist and student leader.

Sarah is a twenty-one-year-old white Jewish lesbian who grew up in Minnesota in an upper-class family with her mother, father, and a younger brother. Her eating problems, which began when she was fourteen, include bingeing, extensive dieting, and laxative abuse; her weight has fluctuated between 130 and 148 pounds. She describes herself as "addicted to my scale" and weighs herself at least four times a day. She links these troubles to "having bad feelings about sexuality in general," pressure to diet, and emotional neglect during childhood. She has cut herself occasionally on her leg and arm when she was feeling suicidal. Therapy, a self-help group for women with eating "issues," and workshops on women's hunger have all helped her be more comfortable with her appetite, her weight, and her feelings. She has recently finished college, is a community activist, and is beginning a master's degree program in social work.

Stephanie is a nineteen-year-old white Jewish lesbian who grew up in a middle-class family with her mother, father, and two older siblings in Queens and Long Island, New York. Her eating problems included compulsive eating and dieting (with a weight fluctuation of 125 to 183 pounds), which began soon after her mother's death when Stephanie was twelve years old. She links these problems to her mother's death, sexual harassment that she associates with going through puberty early, and an intense familial emphasis on dieting. Despite her family's focus on dieting, thinness was threatening to her because she associated it with her mother's increasing frailty prior to her death. Stephanie saw being fat as some protection from sexual harassment. She considers coming out as a lesbian, leaving home and going to college, and therapy keys to learning not to binge. Through therapy she realized she had been blaming herself for her mother's death, which fueled the cycles of bingeing and dieting. She is currently attending a private university in Massachusetts.

Vera is a forty-three-year-old Puerto Rican lesbian who was raised in a bilingual (Spanish and English) working-class Catholic family in Chicago with her father, mother, and three older siblings. She has been eating compulsively for as long as she can remember; her weight has fluctuated between 131 and 200-plus pounds. All the women in her family have "weight issues." She links her bingeing as a child to pressures to assimilate, sexism, and enforced dieting. She ties bingeing as an adult to loss of loved ones, quitting smoking, heterosexism, and fear of intimacy. She has been in recovery from alcoholism for several years. Overeaters Anonymous, Al-Anon, Weight Watchers, and therapy have helped her with her eating. She is currently finishing a Ph.D. in education, teaches at a college, and lives with her partner of ten years.

Yolanda is a thirty-three-year-old Cape Verdean heterosexual woman who was raised in Roxbury, Massachusetts, in a working-class/poor Catholic family with five siblings. She has two young sons and supports herself on AFDC while she is attending college. She traces her compulsive eating and weight fluctuation (between 117 and 204 pounds) to the stresses of poverty, the long-term effects of an emotionally and physically abusive relationship with her ex-husband, and childhood trauma including her father's murder by police, seeing her mother beaten, parental alcoholism, and an attempted rape. She links her understanding of bingeing to going to college and support she gets from family members. Realizing the self-determination it took to leave her husband and make a commitment to raising her children well has affirmed her strength. She is finishing college while maintaining a part-time job and raising her children.

Notes

Chapter 1. Making "a Way outa No Way"

1. The title of this chapter is from Bernice Johnson Reagon's "Oughta Be a Woman": "A way outa no way is too much to ask / Too much of a task for any one woman." The song is on Sweet Honey in the Rock's album "Good News," music by Bernice Johnson Reagon, lyrics by June Jordan (Washington, D.C.: Songtalk Publishing, 1980).

2. Richard Wright, *American Hunger* (New York: Harper & Row, 1977).

3. Susan Sontag, *Illness as Metaphor and AIDS and Its Metaphors* (New York: Doubleday, 1989), p. 100.

4. Sontag contrasts metaphors about diseases in which germs are portrayed as invading the body to the language about AIDS in which people who are HIV positive are considered to have bodies whose own cells are the invaders. Sontag writes, "This is the language of political paranoia, with its characteristic distrust of a pluralistic world"(p. 106).

5. The National Eating Disorders Screening Program Procedure Manual, 1996 (p. 16) available through the National Mental Illness Screening Project. The incidence of bulimia and anorexia is difficult to determine exactly because of problems involved in conducting reliable epidemiological studies and the narrow populations of women included in many studies. For a summary of epidemiological studies on bulimia, see Kathryn Hamilton, Beverly Gelwick, and Charles Meade, "The Definition and Prevalence of Bulimia," in *The Binge-Purge Syndrome: Diagnosis, Treatment and Research*, ed. Raymond Hawkins, William Fremouw, and Pamela Clement (New York: Springer, 1984), pp. 3-26; and James J. Gray and Kathryn Ford, "The Incidence of Bulimia in a College Sample," *International Journal of Eating Disorders* 4, no. 2 (1985): 201-10. Among the studies reviewed by Gray and Ford, estimates of bulimia range from 2 to 13 percent, depending on the criteria used. When strict diagnostic criteria are used, between .46 and 2 percent of young women are anorexic. See A. H. Crisp, R. L. Palmer, and R. S. Kalucy, "How Common Is Anorexia Nervosa? A Prevalence Study," *British Journal of Psychiatry* 218 (1976): 549-54. Based on a number of different studies, between 5 and 10 percent of young women have milder forms of anorexia; see Michael Strober, "Anorexia Nervosa: History and Psychological Concepts," in Kelly D. Brownell and John P. Foreyt, eds., *Handbook of Eating Disorders* (New York: Basic Books, 1986), pp. 231-46. For a discussion of the epidemiology of anorexia in the 1980s, see Joan Jacobs Brumberg's cultural history, *Fasting Girls: The Emergence of Anorexia as a Modern Disease* (Cambridge, Mass.: Harvard University Press, 1988), pp. 10-14.

6. In *Linden Hills* (New York: Ticknor and Fields, 1985) the women's bulimia and anorexia are linked to their isolation from their communities of origin and the sterility

and loneliness of their lives as "kept" wives and mothers. Luz Maria Umpierre-Herrera's *The Margarita Poems* (Bloomington, Ind.: Third Woman Press, 1987) includes descriptions of a struggle with anorexia.

7. For research on food and eating problems in prison, see Nancy Shaw, Martha Rutherdale, and Jo Kenny, "Eating More and Enjoying It Less: U.S. Prison Diets for Women," *Women and Health* 19, no. 1 (Spring 1985): 39-57. See also "What's Important Is What You Look Like," *Gay Community News*, July 24-30, 1988, pp. 11-13, 15.

8. For research on physiological consequences of eating problems, see Paul Copeland, "Neuroendocrine Aspects of Eating Disorders," in *Theory and Treatment of Anorexia Nervosa and Bulimia*, ed. Steven Wiley Emmett (New York: Brunner/Mazel, 1985), pp. 51-72; Norman Spack, "Medical Complications of Anorexia Nervosa and Bulimia," in *Theory and Treatment of Anorexia Nervosa and Bulimia*, pp. 5-19. For research on eating problems as multidimensional disorders, see Paul Garfinkel and David Garner, *Anorexia Nervosa: A Multidimensional Perspective* (New York: Brunner/Mazel, 1982). For analyses of how medical treatment may victimize women, see David Garner, "Iatrogenesis in Anorexia Nervosa and Bulimia Nervosa," *International Journal of Eating Disorders* 4, no. 4 (1985): 701-26; and Susie Orbach, *Hunger Strike: The Anorectic's Struggle as a Metaphor for Our Age* (New York: Norton, 1986). Orbach opposes medical treatment in which women are subjected to involuntary sedation, forced feeding, denial of privacy, total bed rest, and restricted rights to visitors. In her critique of these practices, she writes, "In civilized [*sic*] hospitals throughout the U.S. and England, doctors are perfecting even more elegant techniques to bypass women's mouths and push food into their stomachs" (p. 198).

9. Kim Chernin, *The Obsession: Reflections on the Tyranny of Slenderness* (New York: Harper & Row, 1981); Kim Chernin, *The Hungry Self: Women, Eating and Identity* (New York: Times Books, 1985); Marilyn Lawrence, *Fed Up and Hungry: Women, Oppression and Food* (New York: Peter Bedrick, 1987); Marsha Millman, *Such a Pretty Face: Being Fat in America* (New York: Norton, 1980); Susie Orbach, *Hunger Strike*; Maria P. P. Root, Patricia Fallon, and William N. Friedrich, *Bulimia: A Systems Approach to Treatment* (New York: Norton, 1986). For autobiographical accounts, literary essays, and poetry, see Geneen Roth, *Feeding the Hungry Heart: The Experience of Compulsive Eating* (New York: Bobbs-Merrill, 1982); Leslea Newman, *Love Me Like You Mean It* (Santa Cruz, Calif.: Herbooks, 1987); Heresies Collective, *Heresies: A Feminist Publication on Art and Politics* 21, special issue, "Food Is a Feminist Issue" (New York: Foundation for the Community of Artists, 1987); Lisa Schoenfielder and Barb Wieser, eds., *Shadow on a Tightrope: Writings by Women on Fat Oppression* (Iowa City: Aunt Lute, 1983).

10. Chernin, *Obsession*, p. 110.

11. *Glamour*, February 1984, pp. 198-201, cited in Margaret Andersen, *Thinking about Women: Sociological Perspectives on Sex and Gender* (New York: Macmillan, 1988), p. 196.

12. Maria P. P. Root and Patricia Fallon, "The Incidence of Victimization Experiences in a Bulimic Sample," *Journal of Interpersonal Violence* 3 (1988): 161-73; Maria P. P. Root and Patricia Fallon, "Treating the Victimized Bulimic: The Function of Binge-Purge Behavior," *Journal of Interpersonal Violence* 4 (March 1989): 90-100.

13. Feminist researchers have scrutinized the ethics of an array of diagnostic categories commonly applied to women. See Lynne Bravo Rosewater, "Diversifying Feminist Theory and Practice: Broadening the Concept of Victimization," in *Diversity and Complexity in Feminist Therapy*, ed. Laura Brown and Maria P. P. Root (Binghamton, N.Y.: Harrington Park, 1990), pp. 299-311; Laura Brown and Mary Ballou, eds., *Personality*

and Psychopathology: Feminist Reappraisals (New York: Guilford, 1992); Judith Herman, Trauma and Recovery (New York: Basic Books, 1992).

14. For discussion of why "disorder" is a misnomer, see Laura Brown, "Women, Weight and Power: Feminist Theoretical and Therapeutic Issues," Women and Therapy 4, no. 1 (Spring 1985): 61-71; J. Rodin, L. R. Silberstein, and R. H. Striegel-Moore, "Women and Weight: A Normative Discontent," in Psychology and Gender: Nebraska Symposium on Motivation 32, ed. T. B. Sonderegger (Lincoln: University of Nebraska Press, 1985), pp. 267-307.

15. For inclusionary frameworks that counter these exclusionary practices, see Maxine Baca Zinn, Lynn Weber Cannon, Elizabeth Higginbotham, and Bonnie Thornton Dill, "The Costs of Exclusionary Practices in Women's Studies," Signs: Journal of Women in Culture and Society 11, no. 2 (1986): 290-303; Barbara Smith, ed., Home Girls: A Black Feminist Anthology (Ithaca, N.Y.: Kitchen Table, 1983); Cherríe Moraga and Gloria Anzaldúa, eds., This Bridge Called My Back: Writings by Radical Women of Color (Ithaca, N.Y.: Kitchen Table, 1983); Laura Brown and Maria P. P. Root, eds., Diversity and Complexity in Feminist Therapy.

16. Maria P. P. Root, "Disordered Eating in Women of Color," Sex Roles 22, no. 7/8 (1990): 531.

17. See Angela Davis, "Sick and Tired of Being Sick and Tired: The Politics of Black Women's Health," in The Black Women's Health Book: Speaking for Ourselves, ed. Evelyn C. White (Seattle: Seal Press, 1990), p. 21. While black women develop breast cancer less frequently than white women, their chances of survival are significantly poorer; see Evelyn C. White, Black Women's Health Book, p. 27. See also Sheila Battle, "Moving Targets: Alcohol, Crack and Black Women," in Black Women's Health Book, pp. 251-56; Sarah W. Foster, "The Decision to Really Stop: From the Life of a Black Alcoholic," Sage 11, no. 2 (Fall 1985): 40-42.

18. Historically, psychological research in general has avoided disentangling race from class, which has often resulted in conflating the two—frequently at the direct expense of women of color and working-class women. A recent large study that counters such conflation in an examination of the relationship between race, class, gender, and psychological distress is Lynn Weber Cannon, Elizabeth Higginbotham, and Rebecca F. Guy, Depression among Women: Exploring the Effects of Race, Class and Gender (Memphis, Tenn.: Center for Research on Women, 1989).

19. For a lucid discussion of the variability of oppression among women, see Johnnetta Cole, "Commonalities and Differences," in All American Women: Lines That Divide, Ties That Bind, ed. Johnnetta Cole (New York: Free Press, 1986), p. 7.

20. Susan Faludi, Backlash: The Undeclared War against American Women (New York: Crown, 1991).

21. By trauma I mean a violating experience that has long-term emotional, physical, and spiritual consequences. One reason the term "trauma" is useful conceptually is its association with the diagnostic label post-traumatic stress disorder (PTSD). PTSD is one of the few clinical diagnostic categories that recognizes social phenomena (such as war or the Holocaust) as the cause of the symptoms identified. This concept adapts well to the feminist assertion that a woman's symptoms cannot be understood as solely individual, considered outside of her social context, or prevented without significant changes in social conditions. See American Psychological Association, Diagnostic and Statistical Manual of Mental Disorders, 3rd ed. (Washington, D.C., 1987).

22. Harriette P. McAdoo, "Societal Stress: The Black Family," in All American Women, p. 188.

23. For studies that explore this cultural protection, see James Gray, Kathryn Ford, and Lily Kelly, "The Prevalence of Bulimia in a Black College Population," International

Journal of Eating Disorders 6, no. 6 (1987): 733-40; Veronica Thomas and Michelle James, "Body Image, Dieting Tendencies, and Sex Role Traits in Urban Black Women," *Sex Roles* 18, no. 9/10 (1988): 523-29.

24. Alice Walker, *In Search of Our Mothers' Gardens* (New York: Simon & Schuster, 1983), p. xii.

25. Audre Lorde, *Undersong, Chosen Poems Old and New*, revised ed. (New York: Norton, 1992), p. 142.

26. Georgiana Arnold, "Coming Home: One Black Woman's Journey to Health and Fitness," in *Black Women's Health Book*, pp. 270-71.

27. See Andrea Lewis, "Looking at the Total Picture: A Conversation with Health Activist Beverly Smith," in *Black Women's Health Book*, pp. 172-81.

28. The latitude afforded the singer k.d. lang makes her a welcome exception to this restriction.

29. Barbara Smith, introduction to *Home Girls*.

30. Nedhera Landers, "There's Nothing to Compare with How You Feel When You're Cut Cold by Your Own . . . " *Shadow on a Tightrope*, p. 226. Quoted in Pam Mitchell, "Putting Fat Liberation Back on the Feminist Agenda," *Sojourner: A Women's Forum*, June 1990, pp. 37-40.

31. Thank you to Wahneema Lubiano, assistant professor of African-American studies and English at Princeton University, for identifying this contradiction.

32. Judith Lewis Herman, *Trauma and Recovery* (New York: Basic Books, 1992), p. 1.

33. See "Fat or Not: Fourth Grade Girls Diet Lest They Be Teased or Unloved," *Wall Street Journal*, February 11, 1986, cited in Susan Bordo, "Reading the Slender Body," in *Body Politics: Women and the Discourse of Science*, ed. Mary Jacobs, Evelyn Fox Keller, and Sally Shuttlesworth, pp. 83-113 (New York: Routledge, Chapman and Hall, 1990), p. 109. In a 1985 health insurance survey, 46 percent of adult women across age and race were currently trying to lose weight. See O. T. Thornberry, R. W. Wilson, and P. Golden, *Health Promotion and Disease Prevention Provisional Data from the National Health Interview Survey*, U.S. Vital and Health Statistic of the National Center for Health Statistics no. 119 (Washington, D.C., January-June 1986), pp. 1-16.

34. For studies on African-American women, see Arnold Andersen and Andy Hay, "Racial and Socioeconomic Influences in Anorexia Nervosa and Bulimia," *International Journal of Eating Disorders* 4 (1985): 479-87; Gray, Ford, and Kelly, "The Prevalence of Bulimia in a Black College Population"; George Hsu, "Are Eating Disorders Becoming More Common in Blacks?" *International Journal of Eating Disorders* 6 (1987): 113-24; Andres Pumariega, Palmer Edwards, and Carol Mitchell, "Anorexia Nervosa in Black Adolescents," *American Academy of Child Psychiatry* 23 (1984): 111-14; Colleen Rand and John Kuldau, "Restrained Eating (Weight Concerns) in the General Population," *International Journal of Eating Disorders* 10, no. 6 (1991): 699-708; Paul Robinson and Arnold Andersen, "Anorexia Nervosa in American Blacks," *Journal of Psychiatric Research* 19, no. 2/3 (1985): 183-88; Tomas Silber, "Anorexia Nervosa in Blacks and Hispanics," *International Journal of Eating Disorders* 5 (1986): 121-28; Thomas and James, "Body Image"; William White, Lisa Hudson, and Stephen Campbell, "Bulimarexia and Black Women: A Brief Report," *Psychotherapy* 22, no. 2S (1985): 449-50.

For studies on Latinas, see K. A. Hiebert, M. A. Felice, D. L. Wingard, R. Munoz, and J. M. Ferguson, "Comparison of Outcome in Hispanic and Caucasian Patients with Anorexia Nervosa," *International Journal of Eating Disorders* 7 (1988): 693-96; Silber, "Anorexia Nervosa in Blacks and Hispanics"; Jane Smith and Jonathan Krejci, "Minorities Join the Majority: Eating Disturbances among Hispanic and Native American Youth," *International Journal of Eating Disorders* 10, no. 2 (1991): 179-86.

For attention to Native American women, see Lionel Rosen, Christine Shafer, Gail Dummer, Linda Cross, Gary Deuman, and Steven Malmberg, "Prevalence of Pathogenic Weight-Control Behaviors among Native American Women and Girls," *International Journal of Eating Disorders* 7 (1988): 807-11; Jane Smith and Johnathan Krejci, "Minorities Join the Majority."

Asian-American women are included in Shoshana Nevo, "Bulimic Symptoms: Prevalence and Ethnic Differences among College Women," *International Journal of Eating Disorders* 4 (1985): 151-68; Root, "Disordered Eating." See Maria Root's article for attention to women of color in general.

For a study on social class and anorexia, see Simon Gowers and John McMahon, "Social Class and Prognosis in Anorexia Nervosa," *International Journal of Eating Disorders* 8, no. 1 (1989): 105-9. For a review of the literature cross-culturally, see Bridget Dolan, "Cross-cultural Aspects of Anorexia Nervosa and Bulimia: A Review," *International Journal of Eating Disorders* 10, no. 1 (1991): 67-78.

35. The problems of relying on statistics from these arenas with regard to eating problems parallels the limits of data on substance abuse prevalence among Latinos based on admission rates to treatment programs. See David Santisteban and Jose Szapocznik, "Substance Abuse Disorders among Hispanics: A Focus on Prevention," in *Mental Health and Hispanic American*, ed. Rosina M. Becarra, Marvin Karna, and Javier I. Escobar (New York: Harcourt Brace Jovanovich, 1982), pp. 83-100.

36. Root, "Disordered Eating," p. 528.

37. Root, "Disordered Eating," pp. 525-36.

38. Patricia Hill Collins, "On Our Own Terms: Standpoints and Curriculum Transformation," *National Women's Studies Association Journal* 3, no. 3 (Autumn 1991): 374.

39. Toni Morrison, "Unspeakable Things Unspoken: The Afro-American Presence in American Literature," *Michigan Quarterly Review*, Winter 1989, p. 13; Toni Morrison, *Playing in the Dark: Whiteness and the Literary Imagination* (Cambridge, Mass.: Harvard University Press, 1992).

40. Morrison, "Unspeakable Things," p. 11.

41. Retha Powers, "Fat Is a Feminist Issue," *Essence* 20, no. 6 (October 1989): 134. For other autobiographical and analytical essays on eating problems among African-American women, see Georgiana Arnold, "Coming Home: One Black Woman's Journey to Health and Fitness," in *Black Women's Health Book*, pp. 269-79; Byllye Avery, "Breathing Life into Ourselves: The Evolution of the National Black Women's Health Project," in *Black Women's Health Book*, pp. 4-10; Rosemary Brae, "Heavy Burden," *Essence*, January 1992, pp. 53, 54, 90-91; Beverly Smith, "Looking at the Total Picture: A Conversation with Health Activist Beverly Smith," in *Black Women's Health Book*, pp. 172-81.

42. Root, "Disordered Eating," p. 528.

43. For pioneering work on "fat oppression," see Schoenfielder and Wieser, *Shadow on a Tightrope*; Laura Brown and Esther Rothblum, eds., *Overcoming Fear of Fat* (New York: Harrington Park, 1989).

44. Brown, "Women, Weight and Power"; Laura Brown, "Lesbians, Weight and Eating: New Analyses and Perspectives," in *Lesbian Psychologies: Explorations and Challenges*, ed. Boston Lesbian Psychologies Collective (Chicago: University of Illinois Press, 1987), pp. 294-310; "What's Important Is What You Look Like," *Gay Community News*; Ruth Streigel-Moore, Naomi Tucker, and Jeanette Hsu, "Body Image Dissatisfaction and Disordered Eating in Lesbian College Students," *International Journal of Eating Disorders* 9, no. 5 (1990): 493-500.

45. Streigel-Moore, Tucker, and Hsu, "Body Image Dissatisfaction," p. 498.

46. Beverly Greene, "Psychotherapy with African-American Women: Integrating Feminist and Psychodynamic Models," *Journal of Training and Practice in Professional Psychology*, Spring 1993, p. 2.

47. bell hooks and Cornel West, *Breaking Bread: Insurgent Black Intellectual Life* (Boston: South End Press, 1991), pp. 85-86.

48. Toni Morrison, *The Bluest Eye* (New York: Simon & Schuster, 1970), p. 39.

49. Nancy Scheper-Hughes and Margaret M. Lock, "The Mindful Body: A Prolegomenon to Future Work in Medical Anthropology," *Medical Anthropology Quarterly* n.s.1, no. 1 (1987): 6-41.

50. Emily Martin, *The Woman in the Body: A Cultural Analysis of Reproduction* (Boston: Beacon, 1987).

51. For a theoretically rich anthology that traces how race, gender, and class influence the experience of disability, see Michelle Fine and Adrienne Asch, eds., *Women with Disabilities: Essays in Psychology, Culture and Politics* (Philadelphia: Temple University Press, 1988). For a mother's account of how her daughter resisted medical invasion of her bodily integrity intended to "fix" her disability, see Deborah Samuelson, "A Letter to My Daughter/Myself on Facing the Collective Fear of Being Different," *Feminist Studies* 12, no. 1 (Spring 1986): 155-67. For a wise and animated discussion between a biologist and a social activist and writer about the challenges of embodiment, see Ruth Hubbard and Margaret Randall, *The Shape of Red: Insider/Outsider Reflections* (San Francisco: Cleis, 1988). For autobiographical/analytical essays on the effect of breast cancer on embodiment, see Audre Lorde, *The Cancer Journals* (New York: Spinsters Ink, 1980) and *A Burst of Light* (New York: Firebrand, 1988). On the effect of disability on social consciousness, intellectual life, and embodiment, see Irving Zola, *Socio-Medical Inquiries* (Philadelphia: Temple University Press, 1983).

52. Adrienne Rich in *Of Woman Born* (New York: Bantam, 1977), p. 290, quoted in Martin, *Woman in the Body*, p. 1.

53. Wanda Coleman, "Blacks, Immigrants and America: Remembering Latasha," *Nation*, February 15, 1993, pp. 187-91.

54. hooks and West, *Breaking Bread*, p. 86.

55. Diana Russell, *The Secret Trauma: Incest in the Lives of Girls and Women* (New York: Basic Books, 1986); and Lisa Silberstein, Ruth Striegel-Moore, and Judith Rodin, "Feeling Fat: A Woman's Shame," in *The Role of Shame in Symptom Formation*, ed. Helen Block Lewis (Hillsdale, N.J.: Lawrence Erlbaum Associates, 1987), pp. 89-109.

56. The value of self-disclosure in qualitative research parallels that identified by feminist therapists. In her discussion of black feminist therapy, Eleanor Johnson asserts that self-disclosure is both a valuable and a necessary aspect of the therapeutic process. She writes, "Self-disclosure, on the part of the therapist or the counselor, attempts to balance out yet another unequal power relationship in Black women's lives" ("Reflections on Black Feminist Therapy," *Home Girls*, p. 323).

57. While establishing ties facilitates interviews, minimizing or ignoring differences can do the opposite. In her article on the epistemological and methodological issues involved when white women interview black women, Rosalind Edwards writes, "Differences among women need to be explored as seriously as we have treated differences between women and men. . . . We need to explore how the recognition that there are divisions between women affects actually doing research, and, in particular, the interview situation in which white researchers are asking Black women questions about their lives" ("Connecting Method and Epistemology: A White Woman Interviewing Black Women," *Women's Studies International Forum* 13, no. 5:478).

58. Patricia Hill Collins, "The Social Construction of Black Feminist Thought," *Signs: Journal of Women in Culture and Society* 14, no. 4 (1989): 776.

59. Judith Rollins explains that when she interviewed black female domestic workers and their female employers, the interview guide "was used sparingly, more to prod discussion than to direct it" (p. 10). This method, based on the fundamental assumption that those who have lived an experience know more about it than those who have not, allows unexpected issues to arise. As a consequence, Rollins's transcripts more closely resemble narratives or oral histories than interviews. See *Between Women: Domestics and Their Employers* (Philadelphia: Temple University Press, 1985).

Sarah Lawrence Lightfoot notes in *Balm in Gilead* (Reading, Mass.: Addison-Wesley, 1988), a biography of Margaret Lawrence, that her mother would not tell her a story in a linear, chronological fashion because this was not how she experienced her life. Lightfoot writes, "Once she gets located in time, Margaret needs little prompting. She pauses as she reflects on the many paths converging in her head. She picks one and sets forth. The story gains in feeling and intensity as she proceeds, churning up fantasies, dreams and new detours. If I insist on a literal tale or stop her for the facts, she loses her momentum."

60. Judith Herman, *Trauma and Recovery* (New York: Basic Books, 1992), p. 1.

61. For an insightful account of how shifts in language may be a means to achieve either distance or intimacy, see Oliva Espin, "Psychological Impact of Migration on Latinas," *Psychology of Women Quarterly* 11 (1986): 489-503.

62. The experiences of these women are a powerful reminder that consent forms and discussion about the possible aftereffects of interviews that touch on social injustice cannot guard against pain triggered by the interviews.

Chapter 2. Childhood Lessons: Culture, Race, Class, and Sexuality

1. Iris Zavala Martinez explains that statistics and stereotypes often treat Puerto Rican women as if they were a homogeneous group. In her essay on the economic and "socio-emotional" struggles of Puerto Rican women, Martinez writes, "Such treatment fosters a myth that ignores class differences, racial variations, and differences in places of birth and cultural background, as well as in educational process or language preference." In response to this distorted picture Martinez cautions that "only when the portrayals become richer, more sensitive to the multitude of such interacting characteristics, will the dynamic, complex and changing world of Puerto Rican women come fully into view." See Iris Zavala Martinez, "En La Lucha: Economic and Socioemotional Struggles of Puerto Rican Women in the United States," in *For Crying Out Loud*, ed. Rochelle Lefkowitz and Ann Withorn, pp. 109-22 (Boston: Pilgrim, 1986), p. 112.

2. Elsie J. Smith, "The Black Female Adolescent: A Review of the Educational, Career and Psychological Literature," *Psychology of Women Quarterly* 6, no. 3. (Spring 1982).

3. The country she referred to has been replaced with North Africa to protect her anonymity.

4. Adrienne Rich, "Compulsory Heterosexuality and Lesbian Existence," in *Blood, Bread, and Poetry* (New York: Norton, 1986). Compulsory heterosexuality is supported in the workplace and in families when women are channeled into "women's jobs" that pay poorly, allow for limited vertical advancement, provide few benefits, and are fashioned on serving men (secretary, maid, stewardess). The way that compulsory heterosexuality is enforced is also influenced by a woman's class. For example, while a single working-class mother may need to marry for financial reasons—which makes marriage compulsory—women who are independently wealthy do not have to marry to survive financially. While they may be spared this economic necessity to marry, they may

still be psychologically convinced that getting married and having children are inevitable and natural for all women. Compulsory heterosexuality also varies with generation, ethnicity, religion, and nationality. Women who grew up before the emergence of the gay and lesbian liberation movement of the late 1960s endured an isolation and animosity many younger lesbians have been partially spared. Growing up in a rural community in which there is little or no positive reflection of oneself exacts a toll that is often softened in a large city like New York or Los Angeles. Religious differences also influence heterosexist stipulations. Women raised in Pentecostal or other conservative Protestant churches (Mormon, Baptist, Methodist, etc.), in Orthodox Jewish, or in Roman Catholic families face a degree of rejection and exile from their faith communities that far surpasses that faced by women raised in more sexually tolerant religious traditions (Unitarian, Quaker). Latina, African-American, and Asian-American lesbians not only confront racism among white people—including gay men and lesbians—but also must reckon with homophobia among heterosexual Latinos, African-Americans, and Asians. Finding "home" on the borders of these communities is an intricate process of protecting oneself from oppression experienced in triplicate. See Oliva Espin, "Issues of Identity in the Psychology of Latina Lesbians," in *Lesbian Psychologies: Explorations and Challanges*, ed. Boston Lesbian Psychologies Collective (Chicago: University of Illinois Press, 1987), pp. 35-56; Cherríe Moraga and Gloria Anzaldúa, eds., *This Bridge Called My Back: Writings by Radical Women of Color* (Ithaca, N.Y.: Kitchen Table, 1983).

5. While heterosexuality–sexual and emotional relationships between men and women—does not inherently limit women, compulsory heterosexism is injurious since it enforces men's sexual and physical control over them, is institutionally supported rather than freely chosen, and does not allow for the full range of human relationships. Compulsory heterosexuality is partly enforced within families through a socialization process in which daughters and wives serve their fathers and husbands. In many households, girls learn that their mothers are expected to care for themselves, their children, and their husbands. Female children are typically expected to do more household work and caretaking than is expected of the boys. Enforced sexuality may also include the message that girls must provide for male relatives sexually. Both battery and sexual abuse are components of compulsory heterosexuality in that they "assure male physical and economic access and control over women" (Rich, "Compulsory Heterosexuality," p. 50).

6. Johnnetta Cole, ed., *All American Women* (New York: Free Press, 1986), pp. 15-16.

7. For representative samples of psychoanalytic explanations for the conflicts underlying eating problems, see Robert Lindner, *The Fifty Minute Hour: A Collection of True Psychoanalytic Tales* (New York: Holt, Rinehart & Winston, 1955); John Sours, *Starving to Death in a Sea of Objects: The Anorexia Nervosa Syndrome* (New York: Aronson, 1980).

8. For feminist and medical research that shows that psychological and physiological effects of dieting may lead to bulimia and anorexia, see A. Keys, J. Brozek, A. Henschel, O. Michelsen, and H. L. Taylor, *The Biology of Human Starvation* (Minneapolis: University of Minnesota Press, 1950); Ruth Striegel-Moore, Lisa Silberstein, and Judith Rodin, "Toward an Understanding of Risk Factors for Bulimia," *American Psychologist* 41, no. 3 (1986); Valerie Smead, "Eating Behaviors Which May Lead to and Perpetuate Anorexia Nervosa, Bulimarexia and Bulimia," *Women and Therapy* 3, no. 2 (Summer 1984): 37-49; David Garner, Wendi Rockert, Marion Olmsted, Craig Johnson, and Donald Coscina, "Psychoeducational Principles in the Treatment of Bulimia and Anorexia Nervosa," *Handbook of Psychotherapy for Anorexia Nervosa and Bulimia*, ed. David M. Garner and Paul Garfinkel (New York: Guilford, 1985), pp. 513-72.

9. For research documenting correlations between dieting and weight gain, see Johanna Dwyer, "Nutritional Aspects of Anorexia Nervosa and Bulimia," in *Theory and Treatment of Anorexia Nervosa and Bulimia*, ed. Steven Wiley Emmett (New York: Brunner/Mazel, 1985), pp. 20-51; Lisa Schoenfielder and Barb Wieser, eds., *Shadow on a Tightrope: Writings by Women about Fat Liberation* (Iowa City: Aunt Lute, 1983).

10. D. Garner, P. Garfinkel, D. Schwartz, and M. Thompson, "Cultural Expectations of Thinness," *Psychological Reports* 47 (1980): 483-91.

Chapter 3. Ashes Thrown Up in the Air

1. The graphic comparison of the number of survivors of sexual abuse and the population of New Jersey was made by John Crewdson, "No One Wanted to 'Interfere,' " *New York Times Book Review*, February 25, 1990, p. 3.

2. Ellen Bass and Laura Davis, *The Courage to Heal: A Guide for Women Survivors of Child Sexual Abuse* (New York: Harper & Row, 1988). In Diana Russell's study of more than nine hundred women in San Francisco, 38 percent reported at least one experience of sexual abuse before they were eighteen years old. Of the women under eighteen in Russell's sample, 16 percent reported at least one experience of incest, and 31 percent reported at least one experience of sexual abuse by a nonrelative. When the two categories of child sexual abuse are combined, 38 percent of the 930 women sampled reported at least one experience of incest or extrafamilial sexual abuse. See Diana Russell, *The Secret Trauma: Incest in the Lives of Girls and Women* (New York: Basic Books, 1986), pp. 61, 298.

3. For groundbreaking research on this connection, see Maria Root and Patricia Fallon, "The Incidence of Victimization Experiences in a Bulimic Sample," *Journal of Interpersonal Violence* 3 (1988): 161-73; Ann Kearney-Cooke, "Group Treatment of Sexual Abuse among Women with Eating Disorders," *Women and Therapy* 7, no. 1 (1988): 5-21; Demetria Iazzetto, "When the Body Is Not an Easy Place to Be: Women's Sexual Abuse and Eating Problems," Ph.D. dissertation, Union for Experimenting Colleges and Universities, Cincinnati, Ohio, 1989; R. Oppenheimer, K. Howells, L. Palmer, and D. Chaloner, "Adverse Sexual Experience in Childhood and Clinical Eating Disorder: A Preliminary Description," *Journal of Psychiatric Research* 19, no. 213 (1985): 357-61; G. Sloan and P. Leichner, "Is There a Relationship between Sexual Abuse or Incest and Eating Disorders?" *Canadian Journal of Psychiatry* 31 (October 1986): 656-60; Justin Schechter, Henry Schwartz, and David Greenfield, "Sexual Assault and Anorexia Nervosa," *International Journal of Eating Disorders* 6, no. 2 (1987): 313-16; Lori Goldfarb, "Sexual Abuse Antecedent to Anorexia Nervosa, Bulimia and Compulsive Overeating: Three Case Reports," *International Journal of Eating Disorders* 6, no. 5 (1987): 675-80.

4. A clinical survey of seventy-eight women with eating problems documented that two-thirds had been sexually abused (Oppenheimer et al., "Adverse Sexual Experience"). Maria Root and Patricia Fallon report that 66 percent of 172 bulimic women sampled had been physically victimized (sexual or physical abuse, rape, battery) ("Incidence of Victimization"). Ann Kearney-Cooke found that one-half of bulimic patients were survivors of sexual abuse ("Group Treatment"). Ellen Bass and Laura Davis mention eating problems as a common way women cope with having been abused (*The Courage to Heal*). Therapists who work with survivors of sexual abuse have also documented eating problems as common among their clients; see Wendy Maltz and Beverly Holman, *Incest and Sexuality* (Lexington, Mass.: Lexington Books, 1987); Kathy Swink and Antoinette Leveille, "From Victim to Survivor: A New Look at the Issues and

Recovery Process for Adult Incest Survivors," *Women and Therapy* 5, no. 2/3 (1986): 119-43.

5. Kearney-Cooke, "Group Treatment."

6. Kearney-Cooke, "Group Treatment," p. 8.

7. Maria Root and Patricia Fallon, "Treating the Victimized Bulimic," *Journal of Interpersonal Violence* 4, no. 1 (1989): 90-100. In their definition of victimization, Root and Fallon include both sexual and physical abuse, a categorization that bridges different types of traumas.

8. Iazzetto, "When the Body Is Not an Easy Place to Be."

9. Explaining this phenomenon, Demetria Iazzetto writes, "Once the process of leaving the body has been established as a means of successfully surviving traumatic feelings and experiences it may become one's preferred mode of coping when facing other experiences which provoke or stimulate uncomfortable or unwanted feelings" (ibid.).

10. The eggshell and Swiss cheese images came from women interviewed by Iazzetto and the ashes image from a woman I interviewed.

11. See note 4.

12. Russell, *Secret Trauma*; Gail Wyatt, "The Sexual Abuse of Afro-American and White-American Women in Childhood," *Child Abuse and Neglect* 9 (1985): 507-19. Among the women I interviewed, two survivors of sexual abuse are from upper-class backgrounds, five from middle-class families, and four from working-class families. Seven of them are lesbians and four are heterosexual, a breakdown that mirrors the ratio of lesbians to heterosexual women in the study (twelve lesbians and six heterosexual women).

13. Incest includes comments, exposure, fondling, or sexual penetration by a family member or a child's caretaker—someone who has authority and power over the victim and takes advantage of that position to use or degrade the child sexually (Swink and Leveille, "From Victim to Survivor," p. 120). Including people who are not blood relations in this definition recognizes that what constitutes "family" varies widely in the United States. Incest typically involves contact, but may occur without it; the severity of the abuse is defined not by how the perpetrator uses his genitals but rather by the child's experience of violation (Bass and Davis, *Courage to Heal*, p. 21; Liz Kelly, "What's in a Name? Defining Child Sexual Abuse," *Feminist Review*, no. 28 [1988]: 65-73).

14. Lynda Cunjak, "Real Incest and Real Survivors: Readers Respond," *New York Times Book Review*, February 14, 1993, p. 27.

15. This phrase is taken from the title of Iazzetto's dissertation. See also Bass and Davis, *Courage to Heal*, p. 209 about this process.

16. Although being subjected to enemas is not typically considered sexual abuse, the direct and unwanted bodily invasion led me to include this as a form of sexual abuse.

17. For another account of sexual abuse done for the sake of "cleanliness" see Desi, "Story of a Granddaughter," in *I Never Told Anyone: Writings by Women Survivors of Child Sexual Abuse*," ed. Ellen Bass and Louise Thornton (New York: Harper & Row), pp. 140-41.

18. Swink and Leveille, "From Victim to Survivor," p. 120. This explanation should not be used to conclude that women who have been sexually abused tend toward promiscuity. This prevalent supposition has not been empirically confirmed (David Finkelhor and Angela Browne, "Assessing the Long-Term Impact of Child Sexual Abuse: A Review and Conceptualization," in *Family Abuse and Its Consequences*, ed. Gerald T. Hotaling, D. Finkelhor, J. Kirkpatrick, and M. Straus [Beverly Hills, Calif.: Sage, 1988], p. 272). That some survivors report becoming more heterosexually oriented following an assault may reflect negative self-labeling (taking on the myth that their sexuality

caused the abuse), rather than actual behavioral differences between women who have been victimized and those who have not.

19. This notion that survivors tend toward extremes is explained in Swink and Leveille, "From Victim to Survivor," p. 125. Although I agree with their identification of extreme responses, I don't think that women try to make themselves "unattractive," as these authors suggest, to avoid sexual attention. Rather, attempts to downplay attractiveness are meant to avoid further sexual violation or objectification. The patriarchal blurring of sexual violation and sexual attention requires feminists to be especially vigilant not to confuse the two.

20. For attention to these and other symptoms of possible sexual abuse, see Swink and Leveille, "From Victim to Survivor," p. 125.

21. See Bass and Davis, *Courage to Heal*, p. 42.

22. Iazzetto, "When the Body Is Not an Easy Place to Be."

23. John Briere and Marsha Runtz, "Post Sexual Abuse Trauma," *Journal of Interpersonal Violence* 2, no. 4 (1987): 372.

24. Remaining steadfast in believing his patients would have required him to counter sexist assumptions and examine his own role within the patriarchal social structure. See Louise DeSalvo, *Virginia Woolf: The Impact of Childhood Sexual Abuse on Her Life and Work* (Boston: Beacon, 1989); Judith Herman, *Father Daughter Incest* (Cambridge, Mass.: Harvard University Press, 1981); Jeffrey Masson, *The Assault on the Truth: Freud's Suppression of the Seduction Theory* (New York: Farrar, Straus & Giroux, 1984).

25. See Judith Lewis Herman, *Trauma and Recovery* (New York: Basic Books, 1992); Laura Brown and Mary Ballou, eds., *Personality and Psychopathology: Feminist Reappraisals* (New York: Guilford, 1992).

26. See John Sours, "Anorexia Nervosa: Nosology, Diagnosis, Developmental Patterns and Power Control Dynamics," in *Adolescence: Psychological Perspectives*, ed. Gerald Caplan and Sege Lebovici (New York: Basic Books, 1969), pp. 185-212; Robert Lindner, *The Fifty Minute Hour: A Collection of True Psychoanalytic Tales* (New York: Holt, Rinehart & Winston, 1955).

27. In what may be the first feminist critique of psychoanalytic obfuscation of links between anorexia and incest, Vicki Druss and Mary Sue Henifin tabulated psychiatrists' explanations of the emotional conflict they believed caused anorexia in thirty of their patients, documenting how the psychiatrists ignored evidence of incest and placed the onus on their patients. See Druss and Henifin, "Why Are So Many Anorexics Women?" in *Women Look at Biology Looking at Women*, ed. Ruth Hubbard, M. Henifin, and B. Freed (Cambridge, Mass.: Schenkman, 1979), pp. 127-33. For additional analyses of how psychoanalytic tenets prevented identification of correlations between sexual abuse and eating problems, see G. Sloan and P. Leichner, "Is There a Relationship between Sexual Abuse or Incest and Eating Disorders?" *Canadian Journal of Psychiatry* 31 (October 1986): 656-60; Marlene Boskind-Lodahl, "Cinderella's Stepsisters: A Feminist Perspective on Anorexia Nervosa and Bulimia," *Signs: Journal of Women in Culture and Society* 2 (1976): 342-56.

28. Lindner, *Fifty Minute Hour*; Angelyn Spignesi, *Starving Women: A Psychology of Anorexia* (Dallas: Springs, 1983); Kim Chernin, *The Obsession: Reflections on the Tyranny of Slenderness* (New York: Harper & Row, 1981).

29. In Russell's 1981 study, 95 percent of the incest perpetrators were male. There is a dangerous tendency to obscure the gender of the perpetrator by using such terms as "family abuse," "family dysfunction," and "child sexual abuse," thereby masking men's role and power as the abusers. It is important that the gender of the perpetrator be acknowledged in the terminology and models used for research on sexual abuse. For an

insightful discussion of this point, see Mary MacLeod and Esther Saraga, "Challenging the Orthodoxy: Toward a Feminist Theory and Practice," *Feminist Review* 28 (Spring 1988): 16-55. Terms such as "battery" and "mutual combat," often used by "family violence" researchers, are "at best imprecise, and while there are certainly occasional instances of husbands being battered, it is downright pernicious to equate their experiences with those of the enormous number of women who are routinely and severely victimized" (Richard Berk, Sarah Fenstermaker Berk, Donileen Loseke, and David Rauma, "Mutual Combat and Other Family Violence Myths," in *The Dark Side of Families*, ed. David Finkelhor, Richard J. Gelles, Gerald T. Hotaling, and Murray A. Straus [Beverly Hills, Calif.: Sage, 1983], p. 210).

30. Alice Miller, *Thou Shalt Not Be Aware* (New York: Farrar, Straus & Giroux, 1983), p. 147, cited in Mary Lynn Broe, "My Art Belongs to Daddy: Incest as Exile, The Textual Economics of Hayford Hall," in *Women's Writing in Exile*, ed. Mary Lynn Broe and Angela Ingram (Chapel Hill: University of North Carolina Press, 1988), pp. 41-86.

31. Root and Fallon, "Incidence of Victimization," p. 167.

32. The horrendous barriers to justice faced by Virginia LaLonde and Elizabeth Morgan are two of the best-known cases in point.

33. Louise Armstrong, "The Personal Is Apolitical," *Women's Review of Books* 7, no. 6 (March 1990): 3.

34. Quoted in Armstrong, "The Personal Is Apolitical," p. 3.

35. Cathy Wasserman, "FMS: The Backlash against Survivors," *Sojourner: The Women's Forum*, November 1992, pp. 18-20

36. Wendy Maltz and Beverly Holman, *Incest and Sexuality* (Lexington, Mass.: Lexington Books, 1987), p. 13.

37. Lisa Silberstein, Ruth H. Striegel-Moore, and Judith Rodin, "Feeling Fat: A Woman's Shame," in *The Role of Shame in Symptom Formation*, ed. Helen Block Lewis (Hillsdale, N.J.: Lawrence Erlbaum Associates, 1987), pp. 89-108.

38. One barrier to a multidimensional perspective is that child abuse research has primarily focused on white people (Wyatt, "Sexual Abuse"). Research by Wyatt (ibid.), Russell (*The Secret Trauma*), and Russell, Schurman, and Trocki ("Long Term Effects") has begun to change this troubling limitation. These studies confirm no statistical difference in prevalence of incest between white women and African-American women. With the exception of the Latinas included in Russell's study, there is scant literature that focuses on Latinas and sexual abuse. Research by Judith Stein, Jacqueline Golding, Judith Siegel, Audrey Burnam, and Susan Sorenson with Hispanic and white adults who were molested as children shows that child sexual abuse puts people from both groups at risk for long-term psychological problems (Judith Stein et al., "Long-Term Psychological Sequelae of Child Sexual Abuse," in *Lasting Effects*, ed. Wyatt and Powell, pp. 135-54); these problems may exacerbate socioeconomic difficulties for Hispanics, particularly for less acculturated and undocumented persons (p. 150). We need further research exploring how issues such as immigration, language, and acculturation may affect Latina survivors of sexual abuse.

39. Finkelhor and Browne, "Assessing the Long-Term Impact of Child Sexual Abuse"; Coral Cole, "A Group Design for Adult Female Survivors of Childhood Incest," *Women and Therapy* 4, no. 3 (1985): 71-85; Russell, *The Secret Trauma*; Bass and Davis, *Courage to Heal*, p. 42.

40. To date, neither the literature on sexual abuse nor the research on eating problems fully accounts for how either of these issues is influenced by social forces other than patriarchy. Exceptions include Laura Brown, "Lesbians, Weight and Eating: New Analyses and Perspectives," in *Lesbian Psychologies: Explorations and Challenges*, ed. Boston Lesbian Psychologies Collective (Chicago: University of Illinois Press, 1987), pp.

294-310; Iazzetto, "When the Body Is Not an Easy Place to Be"; Diana Russell, Rachel Schurman, and Karen Trocki, "The Long Term Effects of Incestous Abuse: A Comparison of Afro-American and White American Victims," in *The Lasting Effects of Child Sexual Abuse*, ed. Gail Elizabeth Wyatt and Gloria Johnson Powell (Beverly Hills, Calif.: Sage, 1988), pp. 119-34; and Wyatt, "Sexual Abuse of Afro-American and White-American Women in Childhood."

41. Dorothy Allison, *Bastard out of Carolina* (New York: Dutton, 1992), p. 134.

Chapter 4. Hungry and Hurting

1. Dorothy Allison, *Bastard out of Carolina* (New York: Dutton, 1992), p. 98.

2. By examining these links, I do not mean to imply that all traumatized women develop eating problems. Nor are the particular injustices I describe the only factors that may make women vulnerable to eating problems; some other factors are the loss of a parent, denial of food as a result of famine or poverty, and physiological abnormalities.

3. For definitions of physical and emotional abuse, see Jeanne Giovannoni and Rosina Becerra, *Defining Child Abuse* (New York: Free Press, 1979); David Finkelhor, Richard J. Gelles, Gerald T. Hotaling, and Murray A. Straus, eds., *The Dark Side of Families: Current Family Violence Research* (Beverly Hills, Calif.: Sage, 1983); Eliana Gil, *Outgrowing the Pain: A Book for and about Adults Abused as Children* (Walnut Creek, Calif.: Launch, 1983).

4. For a sensitive and insightful analysis of the characteristics of abused children, see Gil, *Outgrowing the Pain*.

5. Women who develop an eating problem prior to identifying as lesbians may not directly link heterosexism to the origins of their eating problems. Many lesbians go through a heterosexual phase; those who identify themselves as heterosexual throughout primary and high school years may not feel like sexual outsiders. Identifying as heterosexual may protect them from developing eating strategies to deal with heterosexism or internalized homophobia. Among the women I interviewed, two lesbians were married and several others identified as heterosexual or asexual at least through high school prior to discovering their lesbian identities.

6. Andrew Kopkind, "The Gay Moment," *Nation*, May 3, 1993, pp. 577-602.

7. For discussion linking heterosexism and alcohol abuse, see Kathleen O'Halleran Glaus, "Alcoholism, Chemical Dependency, and the Lesbian Client," *Women and Therapy* 8, nos. 1 and 2 (1989): 131-43.

8. William Bennett and Joel Gurin, *The Dieter's Dilemma: Eating Less and Weighing More* (New York: Basic Books, 1982); David Garner, Wendi Rockert, Marion Olmsted, Craig Johnson, and Donald Coscina, "Psychoeducational Principles in the Treatment of Bulimia and Anorexia Nervosa," in *Handbook of Psychotherapy for Anorexia Nervosa and Bulimia*, ed. David Garner and Paul E. Garfinkel (New York: Guilford, 1985), pp. 513-72; Valerie Smead, "Eating Behaviors Which May Lead to and Perpetuate Anorexia Nervosa, Bulimarexia and Bulimia," *Women and Therapy* 3, no. 2 (Summer 1984): 37-49.

9. Gil, *Outgrowing the Pain*.

10. For groundbreaking research chronicling the psychological and social stresses of poverty, see Deborah Belle, ed., *Lives in Stress: Women and Depression* (Beverly Hills, Calif.: Sage, 1982). See also Margaret C. Simms and Julianne M. Malveaux, eds., *Slipping through the Cracks: The Status of Black Women* (New Brunswick, N.J.: Transaction, 1986); and Opal Palmer Adisa, "Rocking in the Sunlight: Stress and Black Women," in *The Black Women's Health Book: Speaking for Ourselves*, ed. Evelyn C.

White (Seattle: Seal Press, 1990), pp. 11-14; Elizabeth Higginbotham, "We Were Never on a Pedestal: Women of Color Continue to Struggle with Poverty, Racism, and Sexism," in *For Crying Out Loud*, ed. Rochelle Lefkowitz and Ann Withorn (Boston: Pilgrim, 1986), pp. 97-109.

11. Byllye Avery, "Breathing Life into Ourselves: The Evolution of the National Black Women's Health Project," in *Black Women's Health Book*, p. 7.

12. As an adult she went to a library seeking information about his death in back issues of the *Boston Globe* but was unable to find anything useful. While the deaths of white men and women had made the front pages, there was no mention of her father's death, a reality that reflected both racial inequities and police power.

13. B. Wolf, "The Impact of Socio-environmental Stress on the Mental Health of Low-Income Mothers," unpublished qualifying paper, Harvard Graduate School of Education, as cited in Deborah Belle, "Inequality and Mental Health: Low Income and Minority Women," in *Women and Mental Health Policy*, ed. Lenore E. Walker (Beverly Hills, Calif.: Sage, 1984), pp. 135-50.

14. Adrienne Rich, "Resisting Amnesia: History and Personal Life," *Blood, Bread, and Poetry* (New York: Norton, 1986), p. 142.

15. Robert Blauner, "Colonized and Immigrant Minorities," in *Majority and Minority: Dynamics of Race and Ethnicity in American Life*, ed. Norman Yetman (Boston: Allyn and Bacon, 1982), pp. 290-300.

16. Oliva Espin, "Cultural and Historical Influences on Sexuality in Hispanic/Latin Women," in *All American Women: Lines that Divide, Ties that Bind*, ed. Johnnetta B. Cole (New York: Free Press, 1986), pp. 272-84.

17. Durhane Wong-Rieger and Diana Quintana, "Comparative Acculturation of Southeast Asian and Hispanic Immigrants and Sojourners," *Journal of Cross-Cultural Psychology* 18, no. 3 (September 1987): 346. For social theory on ethnicity and assimilation, see Nathan Glazer and Daniel Patrick Moynihan, *Beyond the Melting Pot: The Negros, Puerto Ricans, Jews, Italians and Irish of New York City* (Cambridge, Mass.: MIT Press, 1973). For critical examinations of the melting pot theory, see Edwin Randolph Parson, "Ethnicity and Traumatic Stress: The Intersecting Point in Psychotherapy," in *Trauma and Its Wake*, ed. Charles Figley (New York: Brunner/Mazel, 1985), pp. 314-38; Michael Omi and Howard Winant, *Racial Formation in the United States* (New York: Routledge, 1986); Blauner, "Colonized and Immigrant Minorities."

18. See Cynthia Bulik, "Eating Disorders in Immigrants: Two Case Reports," *International Journal of Eating Disorders* 6, no. 1 (1987): 133-41; Oliva Espin, "Psychological Impact of Migration on Latinas," *Psychology of Women Quarterly* 11 (1987): 489-503.

19. Espin, "Cultural and Historical Influences," p. 275.

20. See Lillian Comas-Díaz, "Feminist Therapy with Hispanic/Latina Women: Myth or Reality?" *Women and Therapy* 6, no. 4 (1987): 745-73; Guadalupe Gibson, "Hispanic Women: Stress and Mental Health Issues," *Women and Therapy* 2, no. 2/3 (Summer/Fall 1983): 113-33.

21. See Shelle Colen, "With Respect and Feelings: Voices of West Indian Child Care and Domestic Workers in New York City," in *All American Women*; Annette Fuentes and Barbara Ehrenreich, *Women in the Global Factory* (Boston: South End Press, 1984); Gibson, "Hispanic Women"; June Nash, "The Impact of the Changing International Division of Labor on Different Sectors of the Labor Force," in *Women, Men and the International Division of Labor* (Albany, N.Y.: Albany State University Press, 1983); Makeda Silvera, *Silenced* (Ontario, Canada: Williams-Wallace, 1983).

22. For emerging research on this connection, see Maria P. P. Root, "Disordered Eating in Women of Color," *Sex Roles* 22, no. 7/8 (1990): 525-36; Tomas Silber, "An-

orexia Nervosa in Blacks and Hispanics," *International Journal of Eating Disorders* 5, no. 1 (1986): 121-28; Bulik, "Eating Disorders in Immigrants"; Barry Dym, "Eating Disorders and the Family: A Model for Intervention," in *Theory and Treatment of Anorexia Nervosa and Bulimia: Biomedical, Sociocultural and Psychological Perspectives*, ed. Steven Wiley Emmett (New York: Brunner/Mazel, 1985), pp. 174-93. For discussion of connections between drug abuse and the stress of acculturation, see David Santisteban and Jose Szapocznik, "Substance Abuse Disorders Among Hispanics: A Focus on Prevention," in *Mental Health and Hispanic Americans*, ed. Rosina M. Becerra, Marvin Karno, and Javier I. Escobar (New York: Harcourt Brace Jovanovich, 1982), pp. 83-100; Melvin Delgado, "Hispanic Adolescents and Substance Abuse: Implications for Research, Treatment and Prevention," in *Ethnic Issues in Adolescent Mental Health*, ed. Arlene Rubin Stiffman and Larry Davis (Newbury Park, Calif.: Sage, 1990), pp. 303-22.

23. In case studies of immigrant women who develop anorexia and bulimia, Cynthia Bulik identifies a family's decision to immigrate without consulting their daughter as a factor related to the daughter's eating problems. See Bulik, "Eating Disorders in Immigrants."

24. Oliva Espin writes, "When a migrant comes from a country where she belongs to the racial majority or where, as in Latin countries, racial mixtures are the norm, the experience of turning into a minority in the United States and encountering overt racial discrimination becomes a disorienting experience" ("Psychological Impact of Migration on Latinas," p. 493).

25. Bulik, "Eating Disorders in Immigrants."

26. Some theorists have noted that many Latinas describe emotional and physical concerns in an integrated fashion. Julianna described her bulimia as both a physiological symptom (a nervous stomach) and a response to emotional pain (anger and feeling upset). Her bulimia was a symptom of stress that she articulated in this holistic manner. One of the stereotypes in clinical/therapeutic literature is that Latinas are not psychologically oriented and describe symptoms of illness only in somatic terms. In her work with Latinas, Lillian Comas-Díaz, a feminist Latina psychotherapist, found that, in fact, Latinas understand a body-mind interrelationship and present complaints that are consistent with "their holistic approach to health and illness" ("Feminist Therapy with Hispanic/Latina Women," p. 51). In regard to the stress of acculturation experienced by Hispanic women, new knowledge about the physical effects of stress substantiates Hispanic women's tradition of explaining illness in both physical and psychological terms (Gibson, "Hispanic Women: Stress and Mental Health Issues," p. 128).

27. Espin, "Psychological Impact of Migration on Latinas," p. 496.

28. Ibid., p. 498.

29. For example: one woman's bulimia began when she was being sexually abused by a male relative and subsided when the abuse ended. She began to binge and diet again a few years later when she was struggling against heterosexist pressures to marry (a psychic intrusion) and the expectation that she have heterosexual sex (which involves physical intrusion). Both physical and psychic abuse brought on her eating problems.

30. Elba I. Crespo, "Racism and Oppression: Expanding Our Definition of Violence," unpublished paper, 1990.

31. Ibid.

32. She may, then, have a hard time distinguishing between her own and others' feelings and opinions and blame herself for things that are actually others' fault. For many traumatized women, no boundaries have taken the place of fluid ones—a negative consequence of the socialization process in which girls are taught to develop incorporative and expansive boundaries. Although feminist psychological theory has countered the tendency to deem women's development inferior to men's, this theory also runs the risk

of romanticizing women's fluid and flexible boundaries. These boundaries may, in fact, make it more difficult for women to protect themselves from trauma than if they were taught the singular and rigid boundaries associated with male socialization.

Chapter 5. A Thousand Hungers

1. Edna St. Vincent Millay, "Who Hurt You So, My Dear?" *Collected Poems*, ed. Norma Millay (New York: Harper & Row, 1956), p. 487.

2. For a lucid discussion of the brain chemicals, serotonin and endorphins, that are released during a binge and promote relaxation and calm, see Anne Katherine, *Anatomy of a Food Addiction: The Brain Chemistry of Overeating* (New York: Prentice-Hall, 1991).

3. Jean Kinney and Gwen Leaton, *Loosening the Grip: A Handbook of Alcohol Information* (St. Louis: Mosby, 1978), pp. 101-2.

4. Mary de Young, "Self-Injurious Behavior in Incest Victims: A Research Note," *Child Welfare* 16, no. 8 (November/December 1982): 579; Coral Cole, "A Group Design for Adult Female Survivors of Childhood Incest," *Women and Therapy* 4, no. 3 (1985): 71.

5. Ellen Bass, "In the Truth Itself, There Is Healing," in *I Never Told Anyone: Writings by Women Survivors of Child Sexual Abuse*, ed. Ellen Bass and Louise Thornton (New York: Harper & Row, 1988), p. 48.

6. Lillian Comas-Díaz, "Feminist Therapy with Hispanic/Latina Women: Myth or Reality?" *Women and Therapy* 6, no. 4 (1987): 39-63."

7. Oliva Espin, "Cultural and Historical Influences on Sexuality in Hispanic/Latin Women," in *All American Women: Lines That Divide, Ties That Bind*, ed. Johnnetta Cole (New York: Free Press, 1986), p. 275.

8. Edna St. Vincent Millay, "Who Hurt You So?"

9. Bridgett Davis, "Speaking of Grief: Today I Feel Real Low, I Hope You Understand," in *The Black Women's Health Book: Speaking for Ourselves*, ed. Evelyn C. White (Seattle: Seal Press, 1990), p. 220.

10. Adrienne Rich, "Resisting Amnesia: History and Personal Life," in *Blood, Bread, and Poetry* (New York: Norton, 1986), 136-55.

11. For discussion of food addiction as genetically influenced, see Judi Hollis, *Fat Is a Family Affair* (New York: Harper, 1985), and Anne Katherine, *Anatomy of a Food Addiction*.

12. I am avoiding the question of the extent to which some eating problems may be genetically influenced. This is a complicated question that, to my mind, involves a level of sophistication about the interface between biology and culture that we have not yet reached. It seems fruitless to consider the possibility that some people may be born with a susceptibility to addiction outside of historical, cultural, and familial influences.

13. For example, Ruthie's purging and dieting began when she was being sexually abused, but when the abuse stopped she stopped purging. Her worries about being fat and her fear of eating also subsided, which she attributes to the emergence of her lesbian identity. After her mother learned that Ruthie was having a relationship with a woman, her mother beat her severely, making it increasingly difficult for Ruthie to live at home. Soon after, Ruthie married, primarily to escape her mother's abuse. Her attempt to be heterosexual and her unhappiness in this role brought on dieting, bingeing, and an exaggerated perception of her body size. These problems continued until she left her husband three years later and became sexually involved with a woman. At this point, her

eating problems diminished again; as before, they were specific responses to stress that subsided when the stress was resolved.

14. Tracy Robinson and Janie Victoria Ward, "A Belief in Self Far Greater than Any-one's Disbelief: Cultivating Resistance among African-American Female Adolescents," *Women and Therapy* 11, no. 3/4 (1991): 89.

15. The distinction between resistance and liberation calls into question parallels drawn between political activists who go on hunger strikes and women who die of an-orexia. A collective hunger strike meant to attract public attention is decidedly different from a woman starving to death in isolation; we must guard against a conflation that masks her isolation. For writing that draws these parallels, see Susie Orbach, *Hunger Strike: The Anorectic's Struggle as a Metaphor for Our Age* (New York: Norton, 1986); Maud Ellmann, *The Hunger Artists: Starving, Writing, and Imprisonment* (Cambridge, Mass.: Harvard University Press, 1993).

16. Ann Kearney-Cooke, "Group Treatment of Sexual Abuse among Women with Eating Disorders," *Women and Therapy* 7, no. 1 (1988): 12.

Chapter 6. In the Mourning There Is Light

1. *A Burst of Light* (New York: Firebrand, 1988), p. 55.

2. Cherríe Moraga, "La Guera," in *This Bridge Called My Back: Writings by Rad-ical Women of Color*, ed. Cherríe Moraga and Gloria Anzaldúa (Ithaca, N.Y.: Kitchen Table, 1983), p. 29.

3. For a critical analysis of the medical system's influence in framing the terminol-ogy, diagnoses, and treatment of eating problems, see Becky Thompson, "Women's Hunger and Feeding Ourselves," *Woman of Power: A Magazine of Feminism, Spiritu-ality and Politics*, no. 11 (Fall 1988): 78-79, 82-85.

4. "Abstinence" is not explicitly defined in Overeaters Anonymous, nor is it a cri-terion for attendance since the program specifically claims that it is neither a diet club nor a meal plan. Loosely defined, "abstinence" means learning to eat sanely. For com-pulsive eaters, that means learning when to stop eating and for those who diet, learning that it is okay to start.

5. For insightful critiques of twelve-step programs and the recovery industry, see Sheila Battle, "Moving Targets: Crack, Alcohol and Black Women," in *The Black Wom-en's Health Book: Speaking for Ourselves*, ed. Evelyn C. White (Seattle: Seal Press, 1990), pp. 251-56; Bette S. Tallen, "Twelve Step Programs: A Lesbian Feminist Cri-tique," *National Women's Studies Association Journal* 2, no. 3 (Summer 1990): 390-407; Wendy Kaminer, *I'm Dysfunctional, You're Dysfunctional: The Recovery Move-ment and Other Self-Help Fashions* (New York: Addison-Wesley, 1992).

6. For discussion of how self-help groups (including twelve-step programs) allevi-ate the alienation and isolation characteristic of those with post-traumatic stress disor-der, see Laura Brown, "From Alienation to Connection: Feminist Therapy with Post Traumatic Stress Disorder," *Women and Therapy* 5 (1986): 13-26.

7. According to some people in Overeaters Anonymous, avoiding food that people binge on that is especially "emotionally charged" makes it easier to avoid bingeing.

8. Tallen, "Twelve Step Programs."

9. I say "professed" because, while Overeaters Anonymous, like other twelve-step programs, does not take any stand on outside issues, political or otherwise, the Chris-tian-oriented and male-centered underpinnings of the program are clearly political, al-though as part of the dominant culture they are not interpreted as such. Although OA meetings are attended primarily by women, much of the framework of the program—

including some of the literature and steps for recovery, for example—was taken from Alcoholics Anonymous, which was founded by and for male alcoholics.

10. For an in-depth discussion of the historical and political roots of being an "outsider within" for black women, see Patricia Hill Collins, *Black Feminist Thought: Knowledge, Consciousness and the Politics of Empowerment* (Boston: Unwin Hyman, 1990).

11. This pattern has also been noted among lesbians with alcohol problems. Kathleen O'Halleran Glaus found that lesbians who are alcoholics rarely initially seek therapy for alcoholism. This is why therapists need to know enough about alcoholism to help clients make possible connections between depression and anxiety and an alcohol or drug problem. See Kathleen O'Halleran Glaus, "Alcohol, Chemical Dependency, and the Lesbian Client," in *Loving Boldly: Issues Facing Lesbians*, ed. Esther C. Rothblum and Ellen Cole (New York: Harrington Park, 1989), pp. 131-44.

12. For attention to therapeutic considerations for working with women of color with eating problems, see Maria P. P. Root, "Disordered Eating in Women of Color," *Sex Roles* 22, no. 7/8 (1990): 525-36. For discussion of ethnically, racially, and sexually knowledgeable therapy that is not specific to eating problems but has enormous applicability, see Julia A. Boyd, "Ethnic and Cultural Diversity: Keys to Power," in *Diversity and Complexity in Feminist Therapy*, ed. Laura S. Brown and Maria P. P. Root (New York: Harrington Park, 1990), pp. 151-67; Eleanor Johnson, "Reflections on Black Feminist Therapy," in *Home Girls: A Black Feminist Anthology*, ed. Barbara Smith (Ithaca, N.Y.: Kitchen Table, 1983), pp. 320-24; Beverly A. Greene, "When the Therapist Is White and the Patient Is Black: Considerations for Psychotherapy in the Feminist Heterosexual and Lesbian Communities," *Women and Therapy* 5 no. 2/3 (1986): 41-67; Lillian Comas-Díaz, "Feminist Therapy with Hispanic/Latina Women: Myth or Reality?" *Women and Therapy* 6, no. 4 (1987): 39-63; Lillian Comas-Díaz, "Feminist Therapy with Mainland Puerto Rican Women," *Psychology of Women Quarterly* 11 (1987): 461-74.

13. Catherine Steiner-Adair, "When the Body Speaks: Girls, Eating Disorders and Psychotherapy," *Women and Therapy* 11, no. 3/4 (1991): 261. See also Melanie A. Katzman, Lillie Weiss, and Sharlene A. Wolchik, "Speak Don't Eat! Teaching Women to Express their Feelings," in *A Guide to Dynamics of Feminist Therapy* (New York: Harrington Park, 1986), pp. 143-57.

14. Opal Palmer Adisa, "Rocking in the Sun Light: Stress and Black Women," in *Black Women's Health Book*, pp. 11-14.

15. Thomas Moore, *Care of the Soul* (New York: HarperCollins, 1992), p. 164.

16. Kearney-Cooke, "Group Treatment of Sexual Abuse among Women with Eating Disorders," p. 7.

17. Lisa Silberstein, Ruth Striegel-Moore, and Judith Rodin, "Feeling Fat: A Woman's Shame," in *The Role of Shame in Symptom Formation*, ed. Helen Block Lewis (Hillsdale, N.J.: Lawrence Erlbaum Associates, 1987), p. 101.

18. The origin of the name of this group is a poem by Maya Angelou.

19. That she was the only white woman who drew a connection between healing and race consciousness speaks to how racial identity formation is often most invisible, and therefore unquestioned, among those granted racial power in this society.

20. Kathy Swink and Antoinette E. Leveille, "From Victim to Survivor: A New Look at the Issues and Recovery Process for Adult Incest Survivors," *Women and Therapy* 5, no. 2/3: 127.

21. Laura S. Brown and Esther D. Rothblum, eds., *Overcoming Fear of Fat* (New York: Harrington Park, 1989); Pam Mitchell, "Putting Fat Liberation Back on the Feminist Agenda," *Sojourner: A Women's Forum*, June 1990, pp. 37-40; Lisa Schoenfielder

and Barb Wieser, eds., *Shadow on a Tightrope: Writings by Women about Fat Liberation* (Iowa City, Iowa: Aunt Lute, 1983).

22. For discussion of how the starts and stops in healing are manifested in therapy, see Maria P. P. Root, Patricia Fallon, and William N. Friedrich, *Bulimia: A Systems Approach to Treatment* (New York: Norton, 1986).

23. Dujon, Gradford, and Stevens, "Reports from the Front: Welfare Mothers up in Arms," in *For Crying out Loud: Women and Poverty in the United States*, ed. Rochelle Lefkowitz and Ann Withorn (New York: Pilgrim, 1986), p. 216.

24. See Root, "Disordered Eating," p. 533.

Index

Becky W. Thompson, a visiting assistant professor of African American studies and sociology at Wesleyan University, was formerly a Rockefeller postdoctoral fellow in African American studies at Princeton University. She holds a Ph.D. in sociology from Brandeis University and has taught at Bowdoin College and the University of Massachusetts. She is the coeditor, with Sangeeta Tyagi, of *Beyond a Dream Deferred: Multicultural Education and the Politics of Excellence* (Minnesota, 1993). In addition, she has been facilitating workshops on eating problems and healing in university and community settings during the past decade.